I WRITE YOU RECITE

I WRITE YOU RECITE

POEMS THAT DELIGHT,
HIGHLIGHTS & BRING INSIGHTS TO
EVERYDAY ISSUES OF LIFE

CHARMAINE ALLWOOD HANSON

I WRITE

YOU RECITE

POEMS THAT DELIGHT, HIGHLIGHTS & BRING INSIGHTS

TO EVERYDAY ISSUES OF LIFE

Copyright © 2021

by

Charmaine Allwood-Hanson

Azuri Production

All rights reserved. No part of this publication may be reproduced, distributed, or transmitted in any form or by any means, including photocopying, recording, or other electronic or mechanical methods, without the prior written permission of the author or publisher, except in the case of brief quotations embodied in critical reviews and certain other noncommercial uses permitted by copyright law.

ISBN: 978-1-5323-9742-4

Charmaine Allwood-Hanson

First Printing 2021

Printed in the United States of America

Acknowledgment

I love being creative and imaginative with words. Writing on topical issues, historical events, love, and matters affecting the community and the world at large. Having said that, here I am once again, displaying my creativity with words, presented in my new book of poems titled,

"I Write, You Recite." This book is filled with lyrical, passionate, inspirational, and emotional poems. I do hope you will enjoy reading, laughing, and be inspired by these poems as you did with my first book "I Speak, You Read." Thanks to one and all for the support.

A special thank you to my spouse Winston, who peruses my poems and is honest in his critique. My children Richard, Barrie, and Chaz, for listening and reviewing my poems. They have the honor of being my first listening ears. Thanks also to Georgia Barrett my friend, who often preview and give insightful points on my poems.

A big thank you to Dr. Shelly Cameron, who plays the role of a consultant, mentor, and most of all a friend. Dr. Cameron, always the encourager, constantly prompting and encouraging me to get my poems published. So, I can proudly say Dr. Cameron is instrumental in my journey to authorship, and to her, I am forever grateful.

Thanks to all other family members, associates, and friends who listened attentively as I read my poems.

Thank you sincerely.

Dedicated to my loving husband Winston.

My three heartbeats

Richard, Barrie, & Chaz

And my adorable grandkids

Nate, Jaide, and Queen

TABLE OF CONTENTS

MY WRITING STYLE	1
THERE MUST BE A GOD	3
I AM BLESSED	5
I WILL ALWAYS THANK GOD	7
CHOOSE JESUS CHRIST	9
MY HUSBAND	11
CORONA	14
THE INSURRECTIONIST	16
MARTIN LUTHER KING JR.	18
THE FINAL CALL	20
I AM JUST AN AVERAGE NEGRO	22
YOUR TIME IS UP	24
COVID19	26
MY JOURNEY WITH PARKINSON'S DISEASE	28
SAGA OF GEORGE FLOYD	30
SHE	32
PLEASE DON'T TOUCH MY HAIR	34
OUT OF MIND/OUT OF SIGHT	36
STAND UP	38
FRIENDSHIP	40
MY FRIEND- SHELLY	42

MY FRIEND-GEORGIA	44
DISGUISED FRIENDSHIP	46
LOVE YOUR SKIN	48
THE SLAVE GIRL	50
MR. CORRUPT	54
ON BECOMING A MOM	56
DON'T GIVE UP	58
BLACK INJUSTICE	60
YOU ARE EVIL	62
SAVE MOTHER EARTH	64
OUR HEROINE	66
WHAT'S YOUR LEGACY?	69
SHE IS YOUR MOTHER	71
THOUGHTS OF ABORTION	73
A WOMAN'S CHOICE	76
OUR LIVES MATTER	78
DON'T CRY FOR ME	81
YOU ARE NOT MY FRIEND	83
LAUGHTER	85
NEVER AGAIN	87
DOMESTIC ABUSE	89
OLD-TIME REGGAE	91
SAGGING PANTS	93
ODE TO POLITRICKS	95

BLACK WOMEN	97
OUR HAIRSTYLES	99
FOR BLACK FATHERS	100
THE DECEIVER	102
WOMEN'S DAY	104
WATERED DOWN RASTA	106
YOU ARE A VANGUARD	108
WHAT ARE YOUR INTENTIONS?	110
I THANK YOU, LORD	112
MY MELANIN	113
LET PEACE REIGN	115
NO LOVE FOR YOU	116
MY DISABILITY	117
THANK YOU	119
YOU ARE AN INSPIRATION	120
IS RECONCILIATION POSSIBLE?	122
DON'T TELL US TO SHUT UP	123
WE ARE WEARY	125
I WANT AN EXPLANATION	127
I AM	129
THE WILD CHILD	130
I AM PUZZLED	132
DISCRIMINATION	134
ABOUT THE AUTHOR	137

My Writing Style

I TYPE MY POEMS IN UPPER CASE

NO, I AM NOT ANGRY, I AM NOT INSULTIVE, DON'T BE DISMAYED

THAT'S HOW I REASON, THAT'S HOW I DEBATE

I WISH TO BE BOLD, IT'S MY STYLE, THAT'S HOW I ENUNCIATE

TO STATE MY POINT, TO PROVE MY CASE

SHARE WISDOM, AND BE A KNOWLEDGE BASE

MY WRITINGS ARE MODEST, NOT IN YOUR FACE

AND MY OUTLINE YOU WILL LOVE, YOU WILL EMBRACE

THAT'S HOW I EXPRESS MY WORDS AND

MY PHRASE

I MUST SAY, FROM LOWER CASE I REFRAIN

I DON'T WRITE FOR THE PRAISE, IT IS JUST MY UNIQUE WAY

TO VERBALIZE WHAT I SAY, AND MY INTENTIONS CONVEY

I AM NOT MUNDANE, MY LYRICS ARE NOT PROFANE

FROM THE NEGATIVE I ABSTAIN, POSITIVITY I DO PROCLAIM

BRINGING TO YOU THOUGHT-PROVOKING TOPICS TO THE PLATE

I TRY NOT TO DICTATE, I TRY TO EDUCATE

MY CONTENTS ARE TO UPLIFT, MY NARRATIVES ARE HUMANE

I AM GLAD YOU LIKE MY MODE, MY WAY YOU APPRECIATE

THANK YOU ALL FOR READING MY POEMS

AND THE IMAGES I PORTRAY

THERE MUST BE A GOD

DON'T TELL ME GOD DOESN'T EXIST

YOUR DOUBT FROM MY THOUGHTS I WILL DISMISS

DON'T TRY TO PERSUADE ME, DON'T TRY

TO PROVE IT

FOR I KNOW GOD EXIST

LOOK AROUND, LOOK AT THE AIR & SKY

LOOK AT THE BIRDS, LOOK AT THE SEAS

LOOK AT THE LANDSCAPE, LOOK AT THE TREES

TAKE A LOOK AT US HUMAN BEINGS

THE DETAILS OF OUR CREATION, THE INTRICACIES

THERE MUST BE A GOD

DON'T TRY TO CONVINCE ME

WITH YOUR UNCERTAINTIES

TAKE A LOOK AT THE MAMMALS AND

THE ANIMALS

ON LAND, IN THE OCEANS

AND THE BEAUTIFUL AND MAJESTIC MOUNTAINS

PLEASE DON'T COME WITH YOUR TRICKS

MY BELIEF DON'T CONTRADICT
BECAUSE I MUST ADMIT, I DO KNOW GOD EXIST
I REJECT YOUR NOTIONS
OF THE BIG BANG EXPLOSION, YOUR ALLUSION
OF APE TO MAN EVOLUTION
THIS IS NO PLOY, THIS NO GIMMICKS
I KNOW GOD EXIST
AS I WAS CREATED IN HIS IMAGE

I AM BLESSED

I AM FORTUNATE, I HAVE GOOD HEALTH
I OWN MY HOUSE, I DON'T PAY RENT
I ABLE TO PAY A MORTGAGE, I AM CONTENT
I AM NOT STARVING, I HAVE NOURISHMENT
ACCESS TO CLEAN WATER, THAT'S A DIVIDEND
NO POLLUTION AROUND ME
THAT WOULD BE A DETRIMENT
I HAVE AN EDUCATION, I HAVE A JOB
I AM NOT LAZY, I AM NOT A SLOB
INIQUITY I ABHOR, JUSTICE I ADORE
POSITIVITY I PORTRAY, NEGATIVITY I IGNORE
I HAVE SHELTER, I HAVE A ROOF OVER MY HEAD
AT NIGHTS I CAN RELAX AND SLEEP IN MY BED
I LIVE IN TRANQUILITY, NOT IN WAR AND MAYHEM
MY GOD, FAITH, AND BELIEFS ARE NOT CONDEMN
I CAN VOTE, I CAN DEMONSTRATE, I CAN STRIKE
I CAN DRIVE A CAR OR RIDE A BIKE
I HAVE CHOICES, I HAVE CIVIL RIGHTS

MY VIEWS AND MY OPINIONS I CAN FREELY VOICE

I HAVE FAMILY, I HAVE LOVE AND I HAVE

A GOOD LIFE

I HAVE QUALITY ROADS AND STREETS

ACCESS TO HEALTHCARE & THE POLICE

I HAVE FREEDOM, I AM UNRESTRICTED

I LIVE IN PEACE

I NOT WEALTHY AS YOU, BUT I AM NOT A PAUPER THAT'S TRUE

I AM PROSPEROUS, I AM FILL WITH GRATITUDE

I AM SATISFIED, I AM HAPPY, OPTIMISM I EXUDE

TO GOD, THE FATHER I WILL ALWAYS SAY

THANK YOU

I WILL ALWAYS THANK GOD

NO MATTER MY CHALLENGES OR DISTRESS

WHETHER FAILURES OR SUCCESS

DAILY I THANK THE LORD, FOR I KNOW I AM BLESSED

NO MATTER THE TRIBULATIONS AND THE DAMNATION

LIFE'S COMPLICATION AND DEGRADATION

THERE IS ALWAYS HOPE, LORD BECAUSE OF YOUR SALVATION

IF I AM PRONE TO SICKNESS OR DECLINING HEALTH

I WILL CONTINUALLY PRAISE THEE, LORD, UNTIL MY LAST BREATH

IF I AM HEALED OR MARKED FOR DEATH

POVERTY-STRICKEN AND LEFT WITHOUT WEALTH

I WILL FOREVER WORSHIP YOU, LORD, FROM THE EARTH.S WIDTH AND DEPTH

DESPITE IN THE DUMPS AND YEARNINGS FOR A BREAKTHROUGH

I WILL ALWAYS GLORIFY YOUR NAME AND DISPLAY GRATITUDE

MY LIFE MAY SEEM CURSED, AND I MAY BE DEEMED A REJECT

BUT REVERENCE TO YOU GOD I WILL ALWAYS PROJECT

WHETHER I AM IN THE EAST, WEST, NORTH, OR SOUTH

NO MATTER TIME OF PLENTY OR TIME OF FAMINE OR DROUGHT

IN ANY CROWD I WILL SHOUT OUT LOUD

MY BELIEF IN YOU, GOD WILL ALWAYS BE PROFOUND

IN YOUR HOLY NAME I WILL NEVER LOSE FAITH NEITHER BE IN DOUBT

AND I WILL CONTINUALLY BE A FOLLOWER

BE A DEVOUT

CHOOSE JESUS CHRIST

I WISH I KNEW CHRIST

BEFORE MY IMPENDING DEMISE

I WISH I COULD GET BACK MY LIFE

LIVED RIGHTEOUSLY, AND NOT CONTRITE

ABANDONED MY SINS AND BANISHED THE VILE

HEEDED HIS WORDS AND LISTENED TO HIS VOICE

NOT WAITING UNTIL THINGS GO AWRY

THEN MY DESTINY WOULD BE TO HEAVEN

TO PARADISE

O! I WISH I KNEW CHRIST, ACCEPTED HIM IN

MY LIFE

SHED THE OLD, RENEW, AND GET BAPTIZED

SEE ANOTHER SUNRISE, AND OUT OF BED RISE

I WISH I KNEW CHRIST, SPREAD HIS TEACHINGS

EVANGELIZED

MY ADVICE TO FAMILY, FRIENDS, AND ALLIES

TO EVERYONE BE KIND, ACT CHRIST-LIKE

LIVE UPRIGHT OR IN SIN YOU WILL DIE

WHETHER YELLOW, BROWN, BLACK, OR WHITE

POOR, WORKING-CLASS, OR SOCIALITE

HEALTHY, SICK, BLIND, OR ON YOUR DEATH BED YOU LIE

ACT BEFORE IT'S TOO LATE OR DEATH IS NIGH

REPENT, BE WISE AIM FOR THE PRIZE

CHOOSE GOD ALMIGHTY, CHOOSE JESUS CHRIST

My Husband

I DON'T KNOW WHERE TO START

BUT I'LL BEGIN, BY DIGGING DEEP IN MY HEART

AS I AM SO GRATEFUL, BUT I WILL LET MY WORDS DO THE TALK

IT HAS BEEN MANY YEARS SINCE WE BOTH CROSSED PATH

WE EXCHANGED VOWS 'TILL DEATH DO US PART'

NOW OUR TROUBLES AND TRIALS ARE ABOUT TO START

AS SEVERAL RESPONSIBILITIES YOU HAD TO TAKE ON

A DISABLED SPOUSE AND MANY OBLIGATIONS

SUCH AS YARD WORK, HOUSEWORK, PERSONAL AND ROUTINE TASKS

YOU ARE MY GUARD, MY CARETAKER, AND MY CONSORT

FOR YOUR LOYALTY AND DEDICATION, I WANT TO THANK YOU

INNATE QUALITIES, I NEVER SAW AND NEVER KNEW

FOR BATHING, CLEANING, DRESSING, AND TOILETING ME

YOU ARE MY SUPPORT, YOU ARE MY KEY

MY DEVOTEE

YOU ARE MY DRIVER, SHOPPER, BARBER

NURSE AND DOCTOR

FOREVER, TO YOU I GIVE ALL MY LOVE AND HONOR

YOU BRUSH MY TEETH, PUT ME IN, AND TAKE ME OUT OF BED

COOK FOR ME MAKING SURE I AM WELL FED

COMFORT ME, AND SOOTHE MY HEAD

I MUST CONFESS, THAT EVERYONE IS IMPRESSED

WITH YOUR TREATMENT TOWARDS ME AND YOUR ACT OF KINDNESS

TO THE WORLD I DO PROCLAIM AND PROFESS

MY HUSBAND YOU ARE THE BEST

MY CHILDREN ADORE AND SAY THANKS TO YOU TOO

FOR BEING THERE FOR THEIR MOM, TO THEM YOU ARE TRULY VALUED

YOU OFTEN MENTION CARING FO ME, ARE YOUR HUSBANDLY DUTIES

YOUR INTERESTS IN ME ARE CARRIED OUT DULY

YOU MIGHT BE ROUGH AROUND THE EDGES, BUT I SEE YOUR INNER BEAUTY

I GENUINELY RESPECT AND APPRECIATE THEE

MY STRONG MAN, MY CUTIE

CORONA

YOU DISRUPTED OUR NORMALCY

SOME SAY YOU ARE A CONSPIRACY

OUR WAYS OF GREETING HAS CHANGED

SOCIAL CUSTOMS NOW REARRANGED

NOW IT'S A REQUIREMENT TO WEAR MASKS

MANY OBJECT, AND THINK IT'S AN ARDUOUS TASK

NO MORE HUGGING AND HANDSHAKING

NOW WE ARE PRACTICING SOCIAL DISTANCING

USE OF HAND SANITIZER AND DISINFECTING WIPES

NOW A PART OF OUR EVERYDAY LIVES

IT IS THE NEW NORM, NEW RULES TO CONFORM

HOME SCHOOLS ARE THE NEW PROCEDURE

PARENTS BECOME TEACHERS, NO MORE PREACHERS

AS CHURCHES CLOSED THEIR DOORS, WORKING-CLASS NOW POOR

UNEMPLOYMENT SURGING, BUSINESS CLOSING

THE ECONOMY FAILING, THE POPULACE WAILING

LEADERSHIP IS WEAK, THE FUTURE LOOKS BLEAK

POLITICIANS ACTION WE WANT, NO MORE GIBBERISH TALK

NOW THINGS ARE OUT OF CONTROL

OUR LUNGS ARE PUNCTURED WITH HOLES

DESTROYING OUR BODIES AND SOULS

WE NEED VACCINATIONS AND MONETARY RELIEF

AS THIS VIRUS HAS US UNDER SIEGE

CORONA OR COVID19, LEAVE US PLEASE

TAKE YOUR COUGHS, FEVERS, AND SNEEZE

CLEAR OUR LUNGS, LET US BREATHE WITH EASE

ADIOS! MR DISEASE

THE INSURRECTIONIST

ON JANUARY 6TH, 2021

IN THE CAPITOL WHERE DEMOCRACY BELONGS

YOU CAUSED CARNAGE IN OUR LAND

YOU INCITED AN INSURRECTION

CLAIMING NOVEMBER'S 2020 ELECTION, YOU WON

YOU AND YOUR ENABLERS, YOUR MOB

AND YOUR TERRORIST GANG

SHOULD BE IMPRISONED, FOR TREASON, MUTINY REBELLION

AND DESECRATING THE CONSTITUTION

BECAUSE OF YOUR LIES AND MISINFORMATION

YOU STIRRED UP HATRED AND SEGREGATION IN OUR GREAT NATION

YOU ENCOURAGED SEDITION, YOUR SPEECHES ARE LIKE AMMUNITION

THE POPULATION HAS VOTED, THEY HAVE SPOKEN

A NEW LEADER THEY HAVE CHOSEN, YOUR RHETORIC IS LIKE AN OMEN

FROM YOU, THE ELECTION WASN'T STOLEN

WE WILL GET PAST THIS ATTEMPTED COUP
HONESTLY, WE'LL GET THROUGH

NO SECOND TERM FOR YOU, TIRED OF YOUR
LEWDNESS

FED UP WITH YOU BEING CRUDE

RESIGN NOW MR. CONTROVERSY, FOR YOU

ARE UNWORTHY

TO BE PRESIDENT OF THE COUNTRY AND HEAD OF
THE REPUBLICAN PARTY

YOU WANNA BE DICTATOR, YOU ARE A TRAITOR
AN INSTIGATOR

YOU PROMULGATE VIOLENCE, SPEWING
FRAUDULENCE

THE PEOPLE WILL NO LONGER BE HELD IN SILENCE

WE HAVE ENOUGH OF YOUR DEFIANCE

A NEW LEADER IS WAITING AND READY TO REIGN

THEN WE WILL MAKE AMERICA HUMANE AGAIN

Martin Luther King Jr

IN ATLANTA, GEORGIA YOU WERE BORN, IN YOUR FIGHT AGAINST

RACIAL INEQUALITY YOU WERE SCORNED

JANUARY 15TH WAS YOUR BIRTHDAY

NOW ANNUALLY

IT'S COMMEMORATED AS MLK DAY

A LEADER OF THE CIVIL RIGHTS MOVEMENT

YOU FOUGHT HARD FOR OUR GENERAL IMPROVEMENT

INCLUDING VOTING RIGHTS, LABOR RIGHTS

JUSTICE AND EQUAL RIGHTS FOR ALL

IT WAS YOUR MISSION, IT WAS YOUR CALL

YOU SPOKE OUT AGAINST RACISM AND SEGREGATION

ENCOURAGED UNITY IN THE NATION, TO MANY YOU BROUGHT SALVATION

YOU PREACHED NON-VIOLENCE AND CIVIL DISOBEDIENCE

YOUR CHRISTIANITY EVIDENT, WITH YOUR BAPTIST INFLUENCE

YOU GRAPPLED AGAINST POVERTY

ALL YOU YEARNED FOR WAS HUMANITY AND RACIAL EQUALITY

A GREAT ORATOR YOU WERE, IN WASHINGTON

IN 1963, YOU UTTERED

YOUR SPEECH "I HAVE A DREAM" IS ALWAYS HELD IN HIGH ESTEEM

THE NOBEL PEACE PRIZE IN 1964 YOU WON

YOU, THE BAPTIST PREACHERS' SON

TIRELESSLY YOU WORKED AS AN ACTIVIST

AND ADVOCATE

FOR BLACKS, THE POOR, AND THOSE WE BERATE

YOU ATTENDED & LED CAMPAIGNS SIT INS', RIOTS

MARCHES AND BOYCOTTS, YOU WERE A GIANT

DAY AFTER YOUR FINAL SPEECH IN 1968, "I HAVE BEEN TO THE MOUNTAIN TOP"

THEN YOUR ADVOCACY WAS STOPPED

BY A BULLET, A FATAL SHOT

MARTIN LUTHER KING JR, OUR ICON, ALTHOUGH LONG GONE

YOU REMAIN OUR HERO-UNSUNG

THE FINAL CALL

I HAVE REACHED THE END OF THE ROAD

NOW TRANSCENDING AND HEADING HOME

MY BODY NOW DOWNTRODDEN, BEATEN

AND BROKEN DOWN

MY SHIFT IS OVER, I AM READY TO UNLOAD

MY DESTINY HAS BEEN FULFILLED; MY STORY HAS BEEN TOLD

NOW IS TIME, SOON I WILL BE CROSSING

THE FINISH LINE

FOR ME, NO MORE OVERTIME, SEE YOU NEXT LIFETIME

I ASKED GOD, FOR FORGIVENESS FROM ILLS OF MY PAST

I HAVE MADE PEACE WITH MY SAVIOR

NO LONGER AN OUTCAST

MY LIVING WASN'T PERFECT, IT WAS FLAWED

BAD HABITS I GAVE UP AND NOW IN DEFAULT

I HAVE MADE MY AMENDS AND CHARTED A NEW PATH

HOLY GOD I WORSHIPPED AND HIS NAME I EXALT

MY LIFE WAS FAR FROM PERFECT, IT WAS NOT THE BEST

I AIDED THE POOR; I SERVED THE WEAK AND OPPRESSED

PLEASE, NO SORROW OR WEEPING FOR ME THAT IS MY REQUEST

LET ME DIE IN COMFORT, LET ME PEACEFULLY REST

REMEMBER THE GOOD IN ME AND NOT THE NEGATIVE PARTS

TREASURE THE POSITIVE OF ME, STORE IT WITHIN YOUR HEART

MY JOURNEY IS ENDING, FINALLY, I MUST DEPART

REMEMBER MY LOVED ONES, I LOVED YOU ALL

GOODBYE FOR NOW, AS I APPROACH MY FINAL CURTAIN CALL

I AM JUST AN AVERAGE NEGRO

I AM JUST AN AVERAGE NEGRO

INTELLECTUALLY I REASON

RATIONALLY I FLOW

I AM AN OPTIMISTIC PERSON

POSITIVE VIBES I FOLLOW

I AM JUST AN AVERAGE NEGRO

HATRED FROM MY THOUGHTS I DISAVOW

MENTALITY OF WILLIE LYNCH WITHIN

MY MIND IS NOT ALLOWED

RETURN TO THE ERA OF JIM CROW

MUST BE DISALLOWED

HARMONY AND UNITY IS A BEAUTIFUL COMBO

IN MY MIDST THOSE WORDS ARE MY MANIFESTO

I AM JUST AN AVERAGE NEGRO

I AM FOREVER GRATEFUL, GRATITUDE IS

MY MOTTO

YESTERDAY, TODAY, AND TOMORROW

I THANK GOD DAILY, FOR MY CUP OVERFLOWS

LOVE IS MY RELIGION, TO PEACE I VOWED

POSITIVITY IS MY MANTRA, IN SELF PITY I DON'T WALLOW

I AM TRUTHFUL, I AM OPEN, I AM NOT INCOGNITO

I AM HELPFUL, I AM KIND, I DISPLAY BRAVADO

I AM SINCERE, I AM REAL, NOT A PLACEBO

I AM NOT A CELEBRITY, I AM NOT A HERO

I AM JUST AN AVERAGE NEGRO

Your Time Is Up

YOUR TIME IS UP, MR. TRUMP

IT'S TIME TO GET OUT

EAGERLY WE ARE WAITING, WE HAVE STARTED TO COUNT-DOWN

TIRED OF YOUR WHINING, WE ARE TIRED OF SEEING YOUR POUTS

WE ARE FED UP WITH YOUR ANTICS AND OBSCENE OUTBURSTS

WE WANT NO MORE FIRINGS FROM YOUR TWITTER ACCOUNT

ACCEPT THE ELECTION RESULTS AND STOP DEMANDING A RECOUNT

THE MASSES HAS SPOKEN, PLEASE CHECKOUT

YOUR ACTIONS ARE HERETIC, NO MORE OF YOUR RHETORIC

YOU FAILED TO TAKE CONTROL AND CURB THE PANDEMIC

A DIVIDER YOU ARE, JUST PLAIN PROBLEMATIC

THE NATION IS DISGRUNTLED WITH YOUR DRAMATICS

WE WANT AMERICA TO BE ON TOP AGAIN, INSTEAD OF WHITTLING AWAY

ACCEPTING OF REFUGEES AND IMMIGRANTS

EASING THEIR PAIN

BRING STABILITY TO DACA RECIPIENTS WHOSE LIVES ARE IN DISARRAY

BEFORE YOU DEPART GIVE US OUR STIMULUS CHEQUES

WE NEED TO PAY OUR BILLS, MORTGAGES AND RENT

TO EASE OUR BURDEN AND ONCE AGAIN BE CONTENT

AID SMALL BUSINESS AND GIVE UNEMPLOYMENT RELIEFS

THE WHOLE COUNTRY IS SUFFERING AND IN DEEP GRIEF

TO THE WORLD YOU ARE A DISGRACE, YOUR LEADERSHIP IS WEAK

NO TWO TERM FOR YOU, YOUR REIGN WILL BE BRIEF

WE NO LONGER HAVE FAITH IN YOU, YOU'VE SHATTERED OUR BELIEFS

A NEW LEADER WE'VE CHOSEN AS WE TURN A NEW LEAF

THE POPULACE HAS VOTED; YOU ARE NO LONGER COMMANDER-IN-CHIEF

Covid19

WHY ARE YOU CREATING HAVOC AND FEAR?

UPSTAGING OUR LIVES, PLUNGING IT IN DESPAIR

IN 2019 YOU WERE CREATED

THEN YOU APPEARED EVERYWHERE

NOW IS 2020 AND YOU ARE STILL HERE

RAVAGING OUR WORLD, YOU ARE A NIGHTMARE

TO THE 1918 SPANISH FLU, YOU ARE OFTEN COMPARED

LABELLED A PANDEMIC, A NOVEL VIRUS, AND THE PLAGUE

I DO HOPE BY 2021 YOU WILL DISAPPEAR

AROUND THE WORLD YOU GO KILLING MILLIONS

DEPOPULATING POOR AND RICH NATIONS, WIPING OUT GENERATIONS

CREATING HEALTH WAVES AND HEALTH DYNAMICS

TARGETING CERTAIN DEMOGRAPHICS, MAINLY BLACKS, AND HISPANICS

ESPECIALLY THOSE WITH OBESITY AND UNDERLYING DISEASE

YOU ARE DESTRUCTIVE, BRINGING US TO OUR KNEES

OUR LIVES YOU HAVE CHANGED, A NEW NORMAL YOU DICTATE

AS HEALTH PRACTITIONERS TRY TO MITIGATE

WE CITIZENS MUST PLAY OUR PART

WE'LL WEAR OUR MASKS, STAND 6 FEET APART

PREVENTING THE DEATH RATE TO GO UP THE CHARTS

WE WILL WASH OUR HANDS AND AVOID THE INFECTED

GET TESTED, KEEP OUR SURROUNDINGS DISINFECTED

SANITIZE, QUARANTINE, AND VIRTUALLY SOCIALIZE

NOW CHILDREN ARE HOMESCHOOLING, BUSINESS CLOSING

INDUSTRIES FOLDING, HOMELESSNESS GROWING

RELATIONSHIPS CORRODING, TEMPERS EXPLODING

COVID19 IT'S YOU, I AM DISCUSSING

TO THE DOUBTERS, CRITICS, AND SKEPTICS

COVID19 IS REAL, IT'S WORLDWIDE, IT'S EPIC

GOD BLESS US ALL DURING THIS PANDEMIC

My Journey with Parkinson's Disease

I HAD HOPES, I HAD DREAMS

NOW I AM AFFLICTED WITH THIS DEBILITATING DISEASE

I CAN'T MOVE OM MY OWN, I CANNOT SLEEP

I CAN'T WALK, IT AFFECTS MY SPEECH

I HAD HOPES, I HAD DREAMS

I HAVE TO BE FED, MY FEET ARE HEAVY AS LEAD

I GET AID WITH BATHS AND HELPED IN AND OUT OF BED

MY FUTURE IS GLOOMY, IT IS DREAD

MY LIFE IS OVER, IT'S AS IF I AM DEAD

I HAD HOPES, I HAD DREAMS

ALL MY HIGHER EDUCATION AND MY NURSING DEGREES

NOW WASTED, NOW OBSOLETE

I AM NO LONGER VALUABLE TO SOCIETY

I AM BROKEN, I AM USELESS, I AM INCOMPLETE

IT IS DIFFICULT TO CLEAN MYSELF WHEN I
EXCRETE

OR PERFORM SIMPLE TASKS AS BRUSHING
MY TEETH

IT IS WORSE TO HOLD A GLASS OR DRINK
A CUP OF TEA

BECAUSE MY HAND TREMORS, I HAVE
NO BALANCE

I WALK AND FREEZE

I AM EASILY FATIGUED AND I AM WEAK

MY JOINTS ACHE DUE TO RIGIDITY

I SHOUT IN AGONY; I CRY AND SCREAM

I PRAY AND BEG GOD PLEASE

TO CLEANSE MY BODY OF THIS DISEASE

AND MAKE MY LAST DAYS ON THIS EARTH SERENE

UNTIL IT IS TIME FOR MY BURDEN TO BE EASED

LORD SAVE MY SOUL AND HEAR MY PLEADS

I HAD HOPES, I HAD DREAMS

SAGA OF GEORGE FLOYD

PLEASE I CAN'T BREATHE

I BEG YOU PLEASE, REMOVE YOUR KNEES

FROM MY NECK, OR I'LL END UP DEAD

SEE ME CRYING, LOOK I AM DYING

MY NOSE IS BLEEDING, I AM PLEADING

MY MOUTH IS FOAMING, HEAR ME MOANING

YOU HAVE ME DETAINED; YOU HAVE ME RESTRAINED

NO, I AM NOT RESISTING

MY BREATHING YOU ARE RESTRICTING

MY VEIN IS BEING CONSTRICTED

I AM SUBDUED, I AM HANDCUFFED, I AM NO THREAT

WHY DO YOU WISH UPON ME EARLY DEATH?

NINE MINUTES TWENTY-NINE SECONDS, YOU KNELT ON MY NECK

MY PULSE CHECKED, NO CPR TO RESURRECT

I AM SLOWLY DYING, I AM SLOWLY EXPIRING

MY LIFE IS FADING, IT'S SLIPPING AWAY
ON THIS WOEFUL MONDAY
I SAY I AM THIRSTY, BUT NO WATER, NO MERCY
IT SEEMS MY LIFE IS UNWORTHY
NOW I AM BARELY ALIVE, WISH I COULD
BE REVIVED
I DON'T THINK I WILL SURVIVE
THIS IS MY TRAUMA, MAYBE MY KARMA
I CALLED OUT FOR MY MAMA
NOW, THIS IS THE ENDING OF MY DRAMA
I AM GEORGE FLOYD, AND THAT'S MY SAGA

SHE

SHE CHOSE THE WRONG MEN ALL THE TIME

SHE COULD NEVER GET IT RIGHT

SHE LOATHED THE DRAMA IN HER LIFE

SHE THOUGHT THE ABUSE AND BEATINGS WAS ALRIGHT

SHE THOUGHT THE BATTERING WASN'T A CRIME

SHE SAID HE LOVED HER THAT'S WHY THEY FIGHT

SHE WASN'T ALLOWED FRIENDS, SHE WAS IN A PLIGHT

SHE WAS CONTROLLED BY HIM, SHE COULDN'T BE OUT OF HIS SIGHT

SHE SOUGHT HELP, SHE TRIED TO RUN, AND SHE TRIED TO HIDE

SHE ONCE ESCAPED, BUT SHE WAS CAUGHT AND CONFINED

SHE WAS CAPTIVATED BY HIS SWEET WORDS

HE SAID "LET'S REUNITE"

SHE WAS LURED WITH FLOWERS, WINE AND DINED

SHE WAS ONCE AGAIN ASSAULTED FROM MORNING TILL NIGHT

SHE TRIED PROTECTING HER BABIES FROM THE FRIGHT

SHE SHIELDED THEM WITH ALL HER MIGHT

SHE DID NOT BELIEVE UPON HIS KIDS, VIOLENCE HE WOULD INCITE

SHE PLEADED AND SHE BEGGED, BUT HE WAS NOT CONTRITE

SHE WITNESSED HIS TERROR; SHE SAW EVIL

IN HIS EYES

SHE TOOK MATTERS INTO HER HANDS AND STRENGTH SHE APPLIED

SHE DID NOT MEAN TO LET HIM DIE, IN HIS CHEST SHE PLUNGED THE KNIFE

SHE ACTED IN SELF DEFENSE, BUT HER ACTION WASN'T JUSTIFIED

SHE IS NOW HEADING TO PRISON FOR LIFE

HER FREEDOM DENIED

SHE DID NOT LIKE THE CHOICE

BUT IT WAS HIM, HER, OR THE CHILDREN'S LIFE

PLEASE DON'T TOUCH MY HAIR

PLEASE DON'T TOUCH MY HAIR

IT'S RUDE, I DON'T CARE IF IT'S A DARE

DON'T PUT YOUR HANDS INTO MY HAIR

IT'S NOT FOR YOUR PLEASURE, NOR YOUR LEISURE

NO, I AM NOT AN AGGRESSOR, MY HAIR IS MY TREASURE

IT'S NOT A THING FOR YOU TO PLAY WITH AND ENJOY

IT'S NOT A GAME, IT'S NOT A TOY

DON'T NEED YOUR APPLAUSE, JEERS, OR CHEERS

BUT PLEASE DON'T TOUCH MY HAIR

IT'S NOT ON EXHIBITION, YOU DON'T HAVE PERMISSION

I DON'T WANT YOUR PROS OR CONS

NONE OF YOUR VIEWS OR OPINIONS, NO, IT'S NOT A PHENOMENON

I BEG OF YOU PLEASE DON'T TOUCH MY HAIR

I KNOW YOU ARE FASCINATED BY

THE VERSATILITY AND STYLES

THE DIFFERENT ADORNMENTS AND PROFILES

NO, I AM NOT VAIN, NO NEED FOR A FANFARE

BUT ONCE AGAIN PLEASE DON'T TOUCH MY HAIR

PLEASE RESPECT MY SPACE, MY HAIR IS NOT A SHOWCASE

SO, DON'T FEEL, STROKE, OR DEFACE

KEEP AFAR, STAY AWAY, IT IS NOT ON DISPLAY

MY HAIR IS MY PRIDE, IF YOU TOUCH MY HAIR YOU, I WILL CHIDE

I WILL BE DISTRAUGHT, IT'S TRUE IF YOU MESS UP MY HAIRDO

BE AWARE, IS MY STATEMENT CLEAR?

AGAIN, I MUST DECLARE, YOU CAN LOOK

YOU CAN STARE

PLEASE DON'T TOUCH MY HAIR

OUT OF MIND/OUT OF SIGHT

IN THE BLINK OF AN EYE, YOU CAN BE FORGOTTEN

THROWN AWAY LIKE GARBAGE, LIKE FOOD THAT'S ROTTEN

YEARS OF SOCIALIZATION CAN BECOME OBSOLETE

YEARS OF WORKING TOGETHER NO LONGER CONCRETE

ALL THE FRIENDSHIP AND CAMARADERIE ARE GONE

RELATIONSHIPS NOW A PASS-ON

THERE ARE NO MORE TOGETHERNESS

AND STAFF MEETINGS

NO GREETINGS, NO MORE GALIVANTING

OR FEASTING

MY HEART ACHES, MY SOUL BLEEDS

AS THIS AFFILIATION AND NURSING CAREER CEASE

THERE ARE NO MORE CALLS, NO MORE APPLAUSE

NO MORE SECRETS SHARED; NO MORE RUMORS BARED

NO MORE CHATTER, NO MORE LAUGHTER

THIS SEEMS LIKE A DREAM, SEEMS LIKE THE HEREAFTER

MY WORK FAMILY WHO I THOUGHT I COULD RELY UPON, NOW GONE

ABANDON, NO MORE WORK COMPANION

THANK GOD FOR FAMILY AND ASSOCIATES ON WHOM I CAN DEPEND

SHOW EMPATHY, AND REMAIN, MY FRIENDS

FOR, I HAVE BECOME NULL AND VOID ABANDONED, AND CAST ASIDE

NEVER KNEW THAT MY WORKPLACE LINK

MY CO-WORKERS BOND WOULD EVER DIE

FIVE YEARS OF WORK CONTRIBUTION, NULLIFIED

IN MERE SECONDS, IN THE BLINK OF AN EYE

STAND UP

WITH KAEPERNICK

YOU DID NOT SUPPORT OR KNEELED

THINKING HIS ACTIONS HAD NO APPEAL

FORGETTING ALL ABOUT POLICE BRUTALITY

IGNORING INJUSTICE AND INEQUALITY

YOU DID NOT MARCH WITH THE ARCHITECT OF CIVIL RIGHTS

WHO BROUGHT DISCRIMINATION TO LIGHT

DISPARITIES HE TRIED TO SMITE; HE WAS OUR LEADER, OUR SHINING KNIGHT

HIS NAME MARTIN LUTHER KING, HE WAS OUR HOPE, OUR EVERYTHING

THEN MARCUS MOSIAH GARVEY AND HIS CAUSE

HIS MISSION YOU FAILED TO ENDORSE

YOU THOUGHT HE WAS FLAWED, HIS IMAGE YOU MARRED

HIM, YOU FAILED TO ENGAGE, WAR AGAINST HIM YOU WAGED

BLACK BUSINESS HE ADVOCATED, HIS THOUGHTS YOU TERMINATED

THE BLACK LIVES MATTER MOVEMENT YOU CRITICIZED

THEIR INTERESTS YOU FAILED TO PATRONIZE

THEIR ADVOCACY YOU DESPISED

OUR FREEDOM FIGHTERS' EFFORTS YOU OSTRACIZED

I KNOW UNITY IS FAR FROM YOUR MIND

AND YOU ARE RELUCTANT TO JOIN THE FIGHT

BUT THE BENEFITS YOU GLADLY WELCOME EVERY TIME

WHEN WILL YOU TAKE A STANCE? PARTICIPATE AND TAKE A CHANCE

GET INVOLVED DESPITE THE CIRCUMSTANCE

EMBRACE THE STRUGGLE AND REVOLUTION CAUSE ADVANCE

ORGANIZE AND BE ONE, PROUD AND STRONG

STAND UP AND BE A UNITED NATION

FRIENDSHIP

I CAN'T WALK IN YOUR SHOES

I HAVEN'T EXPERIENCED WHAT YOU HAVE BEEN THROUGH

THE MISFORTUNES, THE ABUSE, WITH NO HELP

NO RESCUE

TOUGH TIMES YOU HAVE FACED, MANY TRIALS AND DISGRACE

BUT OUR FRIENDSHIP REMAIN STRONG, IT WILL NEVER BE REPLACED

I WILL BE YOUR FRIEND, WITH OUTSTRETCHED HANDS TO LEND

BECAUSE I AM LOYAL, I AM GENUINE, NOT FRAUDULENT

I WILL BE STANDING WITH YOU UNTIL THE END

I WILL GIVE A LISTENING EAR, WIPE AWAY YOUR TEARS

SHOWING MY COMPASSION AND HIGHLIGHTING MY CARE

I WILL BE A SHOULDER TO LEAN ON, BRING YOUR TRIBULATIONS

WITH OUT-STRECH ARMS I WILL BE A BATON

I WILL BE YOUR LIAISON

BRING YOUR BURDEN, LAY IT ON THE TABLE

I WILL BE AVAILABLE UNTIL YOU ARE ABLE, AND YOU ARE STABLE

I JUST WANT TO BE A FRIEND, MY WILLINGNESS TO YOU I EXTEND

THIS IS NO PRETENCE, RIDE, AND DIE TILL THE END

UPON ME, YOU CAN DEPEND, I GIVE YOU MYSELF

ALL OF ME, ONE HUNDRED PERCENT

My Friend - Shelly

WE MET IN SEPTEMBER 1976

RIGHT AWAY OUR ALLIANCE CLICKED

WHO WOULD EVER PREDICT

THAT OUR FRIENDSHIP WOULD, BE A 40+YEAR HIT?

AT WOLMER'S GIRLS HIGH WE WERE CLASSMATES WE WERE KIDS

ADULTS NOW, OUR SCHOOL DAYS WE OFTEN REMINISCENCE

OVER THE YEARS OUR RELATIONSHIP HAS TRANSCENDED

WITH A LOT OF GOOD DEEDS, AND BAD EXPERIENCES

TEENAGE MISHAPS, SECRETS KEPT

CHILDREN AND GRANDKIDS BRED

AND LOVED ONES UNTIMELY DEATH

HIGHER EDUCATION WE'VE ACHIEVED

COMPARED TO OTHERS WE ARE ESTEEMED

WITH MY BSN, YOUR DOCTORATE DEGREE

OUR EGOS ARE MODERATE, NO SHOW-OFFS

WE MUST AGREE

WRITERS WE BOTH ARE, YOU ARE THE SUPERSTAR

EIGHT BOOKS YOU HAVE AUTHORED SO FAR

INTO BUDDING PROFESSIONALS, WE HAVE BLOSSOMED

WE BOTH ADVANCED TO THE TOP, FROM ROCK BOTTOM

I KNEW JEAN YOUR MOM, YOU KNEW MY MOM MIRIAM

YES! WE HAVE SO MUCH HISTORY

JOY, MISERY, AND VICTORIES

SEE OUR FRIENDSHIP IS SENTIMENTAL

LOYALTY AND RESPECT, MAKES IT SPECIAL

LOVE YOU DR. SHELLY CAMERON

OUR RELATIONSHIP IS PHENOMENAL

My Friend-Georgia

INSTANTLY OUR CONNECTION GREW
WHEN I FIRST MET YOU
WE UNDERSTOOD EACH OTHER
MOOD AND VIEWS
A SINCERE FRIENDSHIP WE HAVE, NOT TABOO
WE MIGHT LIVE A DISTANCE AWAY
AT TIMES, OUR CONNECTION MIGHT STRAY
BUT WE NEVER FORGET EACH OTHER BIRTHDAYS
WE SUPPORT ONE OTHER, YES, WE DO
WE WENT BACK TO SCHOOL, OUR RN & BSN
WE PURSUED
WE DON'T FUSS OR FEUD, GOSSIPING WE REFUTE
OUR CAMARADERIE IS SINCERE SINCE ITS DEBUT
GENUINE FRIENDS, WE ARE
WHEN WE CONVERSE, NO HOLDS BARRED
WE ARE SUPPORTIVE OF EACH OTHER
WE NEVER SPAR
OUR RELATIONSHIP IS ADMIRED SINCE DAY ONE
WE ARE TIGHT, WE HAVE A SPECIAL BOND

WE HAVE EXPERIENCED MANY TRAVAILS
DEATH, HAPPINESS, OLD AND NEW TALES
BUT WE ARE THERE FOR ONE ANOTHER
NEITHER OF US MUST FAIL
DESPITE OUR DIFFERENT POINT OF VIEWS
OUR UNION IS REAL, WE STICK LIKE GLUE
NO INFILTRATION CAN GET THROUGH
OUR LINK IS STRONG AND TRULY VALUED
YOU ARE MY SISTER, MY FRIEND
GEORGIA, I LOVE YOU

DISGUISED FRIENDSHIP

I KNOW YOUR TYPE, I GOT A TASTE OF YOUR BITE
I FEEL YOUR STING, VENOM YOU BRING
YOU ARE SLY, YOU ARE WILD
YOUR ATTITUDE IS NASTY, IT IS REVILED
YOU CAN'T BE TRUSTED; YOU NEED TO BE EXILED
YOU ARE A BACKSTABBER, YOU ARE
AN ATTACKER
PLUNGING YOUR DAGGER, DEEP INTO MY WOUND
RESTRICTING MY ENERGY, CURBING MY MOOD
BEING AROUND YOU, MY LIFE IS DOOMED
THOUGHT WE WERE PAL, THOUGHT WE
WERE MATES
BUT MY INTEGRITY YOU BASH
MY CHARACTER YOU DENIGRATE
MY PERSONA YOU PUT DOWN, MY IMAGE
YOU DEFLATE
NEVER AN UPLIFTER, NEVER ONE TO ELEVATE
FROM YOU I MUST ESCAPE, I MUST LIBERATE

YOU ARE IN MY PRESENCE TO GRAB AND COLLECT
YOU ARE CONNIVING, MEETING YOU I REGRET
NO LOVE YOU GIVE, YOU STIFLE MY SPIRIT
YOU ARE EVIL, YOU ARE A HYPOCRITE
YOUR ACTIONS I DESPISED, I CAN'T FORGIVE
PLEASE EXIT MY LIFE, PLEASE LET ME LIVE
YOU ARE NO FRIEND, YOU ARE NOT GENUINE

Love Your Skin

HEY MELANATED MAN, WOMAN, BOY, AND GIRL

YOU ARE A CHILD OF GOD, ENTITLED TO BE ON THIS EARTH

DON'T FEEL BELITTLED, DON'T THINK LIKE A "HAS BEEN"

YOU SHOULD NOT BE JUDGED BY THE COLOUR OF YOUR SKIN

SO PLEASE, DON'T BLEACH, DON'T SCORN YOUR SKIN, YOU ARE NOT SIN

DON'T ALLOW YOURSELF TO BE DEGRADED AND BE BULLIED TO FIT IN

SHOW YOUR STRENGTH, PROVE YOU CAN WIN

JUST EMBRACE & LOVE YOUR MELANIN

LET IT POP, LET IT SHINE, LET IT BE YOUR BLING

WEAR IT MEEKLY AND WITH A GRIN

STOP ACTING AS IF YOU HAVE CURSED SKIN

LET IT GLOW IN WINTER, SUMMER, FALL OR SPRING

LET YOUR MELANIN RADIATE OUTWARD AND WITHIN

WITH A VARIETY OF BROWNS, AND BLACKS

YOU ARE PRINCES, YOU ARE PRINCESSES

YOU ARE QUEENS, YOU ARE KINGS

BE PASSIONATE ABOUT YOUR MELANATED SKIN

BE ASSERTIVE, BE POSITIVE, DON'T LET THEM CLIP YOUR WINGS

REVEAL TO THE WORLD YOU HAVE GRIT, FIRE AND STING

YOU ARE UNASSUMING, BUT YOU DON'T DO ASS KISSING

YOU ARE SPECIAL, YOU ARE HUMAN, YOU CAN BE ANYBODY, YOU CAN BE ANYTHING

BE PROUD OF YOUR MELANATED SKIN

THE SLAVE GIRL

I WAS THAT INNOCENT YOUNG GIRL

ENJOYING MY LIFE, ADORING MY WORLD

FROLICKING THROUGH MY VILLAGE

THEN YOU RAIDED, PLUNDERED, AND PILLAGED

KILLING, BLOOD SPILLING

DESTROYED MY FAMILY, DEMOLISHED MY LINEAGE

TARNISHED MY IMAGE

YOU KIDNAPPED AND STRIPPED ME, OF MY DIGNITY

DRAGGED, SHACKLED WORSE THAN CATTLE

I WAS MISHANDLED AND WHIPPED, FORCED ONTO YOUR SHIP

MY INNOCENCE AND MY PRIDE YOU THEN STRIPPED

PACKED LIKE SARDINES ONTO YOUR SLAVE SHIPS

MY BODY PLASTERED WITH HUMAN FILTH AND PISS

TRANSPORTED ACROSS THE ATLANTIC

A PERILOUS JOURNEY SO WICKED AND TRAGIC

ARRIVED ON YOUR CAPTURED LAND

THOUSANDS OF MILES AWAY FROM MY HOMELAND

HAD TO ADHERE TO YOUR NEW COMMAND OR ELSE FACE REPRIMAND

PARADED, EXAMINED, GRADED, AND TRADED

MY FREEDOM GONE; MY LIFE IS NOW OBLITERATED

LABELLED NON-HUMAN, BUT 3/5TH ANIMAL.

TREATED LIKE A PIG, SOLD TO HIGHEST BID

BEFORE MY EYES, I SAW MY FUTURE GONE

MY LIFE SLID

MY HERITAGE AND MY LANGUAGE YOU FORBID

MY RELIGION, MY CULTURE YOU DID NOT PERMIT

TOILED ON YOUR PLANTATIONS

FROM DAWN TILL THE MOONLIT, YOUR COTTON I PICKED

AT NIGHTS I WAS GROPED, HARASSED, AND RAPED

I TRIED TO RUN, I TRIED TO GET AWAY

BUT I HAD NO RIGHTS, I HAD NO SAY, I WAS

A VICTIM AND I WAS A PREY

QUIET I HAD TO BE, I COULDN'T RESIST

OR DISOBEY

ANY ATTEMPTS TO ESCAPE

METED WITH PUNISHMENTS HARSH AND SEVERE

BEATINGS AND AMPUTATIONS WAS INFLICTED

IT WAS THE PAY

YOU FORCED ME TO BE YOUR MISTRESS, I WAS YOUR FOREPLAY

I COULDN'T REFUSE, I WASN'T ALLOWED TO FIGHT

MY INNOCENCE LOST MY ROAD TO WOMANHOOD IN A PLIGHT

I WAS YOUR PROPERTY AND CONCUBINE

YOU OWNED MY LIFE

I BROUGHT FORTH YOUR CHILDREN, BUT THEY WEREN'T REALLY MINE

THEY WERE TREATED AS ASSETS, NOT AS YOUR BLOODLINE

TO MY OWN, A MOTHER I COULD NOT BE

YOUR WIFE'S KIDS, I HAD TO NURSE AND BREASTFEED

FROM MY ARMS MY OFFSPRINGS WERE TORN DESPITE MY PLEADS

SOLD TO ANOTHER PLANTATION, GONE FOREVERMORE

I DON'T KNOW IF MY CHILDREN ARE DEAD OR GROWN

DAILY THEIR SOULS I MOURN, THEIR DESTINY I BEMOAN

THE DAY I WAS ABDUCTED, MY FUTURE ENDED AND I WAS DOOMED

MY FAMILY LOST, IN YOUR FARAWAY LAND I WAS MAROONED

MY TRADITIONS YOU ERODED, MY CULTURE YOU CONSUMED

MY LINEAGE YOU ENDED; MY HEREDITY COCOONED

THE HEINOUS TRANSATLANTIC SLAVE TRADE

A TRAVESTY, CRUELTY, WITH MILLIONS OF LIVES, LOST AND DERAILED

ROBBED ME OF MY LEGACY, DEPRIVED ME OF MY TRIBAL ACCOLADES

THE SLAVE MASTER INSIGNIA NOW MY NEW NAME

ALL I HAD IS GONE, NEVER AGAIN TO RECLAIM

AS I AM NO LONGER A FREED YOUNG GIRL

BUT JUST A SLAVE

Mr. Corrupt

WHY THE VITRIOLIC SPEWING

WHY THE MISOGYNY, NEGATIVITY, AND AGONY

WHY ARE YOU SO CAUSTIC? EVIL AND SADISTIC

WHY DO YOU HATE, GENERATE HAVOC AND DISDAIN?

WHY DO YOU DISCRIMINATE?

WHY DO YOU CAUSE BIAS, DIVISION IN RELIGION?

THOUGHTS OF ANARCHY AND SEDITION

YOU CREATE CHAOS, YOUR ACTS ARE HEINOUS

YOU INCITE POLITICAL AND RACIAL WAR

CAUSING DISCORD DOMESTICALLY AND ABROAD

YOU INITIATE ANTI-IMMIGRANTS THOUGHTS

YOU PERPETUATE PREJUDICE AGAINST OTHER CULTURES

YOU ARE LIKE AN ULCER, YOU AND YOUR XENOPHOBIA

YOU DISRUPT AND CORRUPT, NORMALCY YOU INTERRUPT

YOU ARE A LIAR, A DIVIDER, YOU CONSPIRE

YOU ARE A NARCISSIST, YOU ARE LIKE A CYST

YOU ARE REPULSIVE, NASTY, AND A HYPOCRITE

YOU HAVE TRAITS OF A WHITE NATIONALIST

TRY TO INITIATE SOME POSITIVITY

BRING BACK DECENCY AND STABILITY

GENERATE CIVILITY AND MORALITY

AMERICA IS CONSIDERED TO BE THE LAND OF THE FREE

REGAIN OUR GOLD STAR STANDARD AND SUPERPOWER DECREE

RESTORE OUR WORLD POWER AND DIGNITY

ON BECOMING A MOM

I AM YOUR MOTHER, I AM YOUR MOM

YOU WILL BE MY DAUGHTER OR MY SON

I AM PREGNANT, CARRYING YOU FOR NINE MONTHS LONG

YOU ARE MY LYRIC, YOU ARE MY SONG

I AM HERE TO GUIDE YOU AND GIVE YOU NOURISHMENT

MOLD YOU AND FACILITATE YOUR DEVELOPMENT

GIVE UNCONDITIONAL LOVE AND BE A TOWER OF STRENGTH

FROM ZYGOTE TO EMBRYO, TO FETUS

YOU ARE NO BOTHER, YOU ARE NO FUSS, I LOVE YOU SO MUCH

REGARDLESS OF THE HORMONAL CHANGES, AND THE DIFFICULT STAGES

THIS PREGNANCY I CHERISH, BECAUSE I LOVE YOU, MY BABY

DESPITE MY MORNING SICKNESS, NAUSEA, AND STRETCH MARKS

YOU WILL BE MY PASSION, MY HALLMARK

CONSTIPATION, WEIGHT GAIN, AND FREQUENT URINATION

YOU ARE MY CONCEPTION, MY CREATION

LABOR PAIN, FATIGUE, AND FEELING DRAIN

I EAGERLY AWAIT YOU; I WILL GLADLY DO IT AGAIN

I WILL COMFORT YOU; I WILL GIVE YOU CARE

FOR YOU ARE MY KEEPSAKE, MY SOUVENIR

IT HAS BEEN A LONG ROAD, A HEAVY LOAD, I AM ABOUT TO EXPLODE

THREE TRIMESTER, FORTY WEEKS

UNCOMFORTABLE PERIODS OF SLEEP, SWOLLEN FEET

CAN'T WAIT TO MEET YOU AND KISS YOUR CHEEKS

WHETHER YOU ARE A BOY OR GIRL

YOU WILL BE MY DIAMOND, YOU WILL BE MY PEARL

YOU WILL BE MY WORLD

Don't Give Up

YESTERDAY IS GONE, TOMORROW IS NOT PROMISED

TODAY IS NOW, WE ARE IN THE PRESENT

THE PAST IS THE PRIOR, MOVE ON, WE WON'T DESCENT

THE FUTURE IS NIGH, AIM HIGH, PREPARE FOR THE ASCENT

NEVER GIVE UP, NEVER RELENT

WE HAVE TO PERSEVERE, WE ARE NOT IN A COMPETITION

PUSH ON, WE MUST FIGHT, THERE WILL BE NO INTERMISSION

WITH GOD IS IN OUR MIDST, WE'LL FACE THE ENEMY BATTALION

STRIVE TO THRIVE THAT WILL BE OUR MISSION

WE HAVE TO KEEP OUR HEAD ABOVE WATERS

AVOIDING ALL CHAOS AND DISORDER

VIGILANT WE WILL BE, DESPITE THE BARRIERS

STEADFAST WE WILL BE, WE ARE WARRIORS

WE SHALL BE A POSITIVE EXAMPLE, WE ARE HERE TO EMPOWER

A SHINING LIGHT, ENCOURAGING, AND BRAVE WE WON'T COWER

IT IS UTMOST THAT WE SUPPORT AND HELP EACH OTHER

BRING ABOUT GOODWILL, UNITY, PEACE, AND LOVE

TO ONE ANOTHER

BLACK INJUSTICE

BLACK MALES' LIVES ARE AT RISK OF EXTINCTION

BECAUSE OF SO SOCIETAL PREJUDICE AND CONTRADICTIONS

AFFECTED BY A CORRUPT JUSTICE SYSTEM

WITH MASS INCARCERATION AND FAMILY SEPARATIONS

DRUGS SENTENCING DISPARITIES

UNLEVELED PLAYING FIELDS, INEQUALITIES

BLACK MALES' LIVES ARE IN THE PITS

SLAVERY REVISITS, LOOK AT THE PRISONS

COMPARE THE RATIO, CHECK THE DIGITS

CRIMINAL JUSTICE LAWS, NEED TO BE REVISED

BLACK LIVES ARE IMPORTANT, STOP TRIVIALIZE

THOUSAND ARE IMPRISONED FOR MINOR CRIMES

MANY INNOCENTS ARE JAILED, THEIR LIFES' DERAILED

WHY ARE BLACKS PROSECUTED FOR LESSER DRUG USE?

STOP THE ONSLAUGHT, RELEASE AND FREE THE BLACK YOUTHS

WE MUST ERADICATE OR MEND THIS BROKEN SYSTEM

RESCUE AND SAVE OUR BLACK MEN, FOR THEY ARE VICTIMS

BLACK MALES MUST PLAY THEIR PART, CEASE THE DRUG USE

CUT THE GANG FEUDS, LET GO OF THE GUNS, HAVE A COMMUNITY TRUCE

WHAT CAN BE DONE FOR OUR MEN AND SONS?

TO PREVENT THIS TRAMPLE, THIS CONSTANT HIT AND RUN

THE BLACK MAN HAS BEEN FIGHTING WITH NO SIGHT OF A REWARD

THEIR HEARTS ARE CRUSHED AND THEIR SOULS ARE SCARRED

BASIC LIVING IS HARD, BLACK LIVES HAS NO VALUE, HAS NO REGARD

I AM PRAYING SOMETHING WILL BE DONE SOON

OR ELSE OUR MEN ARE DESTINED FOR DOOM

BLACK MEN REMEMBER YOU ARE PRINCES

KINGS AND NOT FOOLS

YOU ARE EVIL

YOU ARE A PREDATOR, YOU ARE A REPEAT OFFENDER

FROM YOUR WICKED ACTIONS YOU GET A KICK YOU THINK, IT'S A THRILLER

WITH YOUR WEAPONS AIMED AT THE DEFENSELESS, YOU ARE A KILLER

ON YOUR PREYS YOU ARE QUICK TO PULL THE TRIGGER

CAUSING BLOOD TO FLOW DOWN STREAMS AND RIVERS

TO YOUR VICTIMS, YOUR DEEDS MAKES THEM QUIVER

IN YOUR PRESENCE THEY RUN AND HIDE, THEY SHIVER

PRESENT IN THIS WORLD TO DESTROY LIVES

YOU ARE BITTER

A CHEATER, A WOMAN BEATER, YOU ARE ALSO A HEAVY HITTER

THE OPPRESSED, THE POOR YOU ROB, YOU KEEP GETTING RICHER

THE WEAK YOU EXPLOIT, CUTTING IN THEIR SOULS UNTIL THEY WITHER

YOU TARGET THE VULNERABLE, THE DESTITUTE, AND MINORS

WITH A BAD ATTITUDE, YOU THINK YOU ARE SUPERIOR

INFLICTING PAIN, IMPOSING GRIEF, MAYHEM YOU DELIVER

YOUR OBJECTIVE IS CARNAGE, YOUR GOAL IS DEATH

YOU ARE THE GRIM REAPER

YOU ARE WICKED, YOU ARE THE DEVIL'S SPAWN

YOU ARE HEARTLESS LIKE HITLER

FROM THIS EARTH YOU SHOULD BE BANISHED

YOU ARE EVIL, YOU ARE A SINNER

SAVE MOTHER EARTH

AS CITIZENS OF THIS WORLD

OUR PLANET WE MUST TREASURE

CONTROL THE ADVERSE WEATHER

PREVENT WATER CONTAMINATION

STOP DEFORESTATION

FIGHT AGAINST NUCLEARIZATION

CONSERVE THE EARTH FOR

THE ONCOMING GENERATION

HALT FOOD GENETIC MODIFICATION, INHIBIT

SOIL EROSION

THE USE OF PLASTICS ARE LIKE A POISONOUS POTION

DISCONTINUE ITS USE TO PREVENT A TOXIC EXPLOSION

WE MUST PREVENT THE OCEANS ACIDIC SECRETION

AND OZONE DEPLETION

PRESERVE THE NATURAL FLOW OF THE SEASONS

CEASE NATURAL HABITAT AND WILDLIFE
DISRUPTION

MONITOR THE USE OF FOSSIL FUEL COMBUSTION

IT CONTRIBUTES TO AIR POLLUTION

IT ALSO IMPACTS GREENHOUSE GASES

SEVERELY AFFECTING COMMUNITIES OF COLOR
AND THE OVERALL MASSES

CHANGES IN THE CLIMATE SYSTEM, IMPACTS

THE ECOSYSTEM

CAUSING MIGRATION OF WILDLIFE & MARINE
ORGANISM

WE MUST INITIATE MEASURES, TO HALT RISING
TEMPERATURES

FLOODING OCCURS BECAUSE OF RISING

SEA LEVELS

IMPACTING COASTAL REGIONS TO BECOME
UNSETTLED

GLOBAL WARMING IS REAL, ITS' EFFECTS CANNOT
BE CONCEALED

WE MUST ALL TRY TO SUSTAIN, WE ALL MUST TRY
TO WORK

AND SAVE MOTHER EARTH, FIND A SOLUTION

END THE WORLDS' ENVIRONMENTAL POLLUTION

Our Heroine

YOU WERE MYSTICAL AND YOU WERE TACTICAL

SOME SAY YOU WERE RADICAL

TO MANY YOU WERE ALSO MILITANT

AND VIGILANT

I SAY YOU WERE DOMINANT, A MIGHTY WOMAN

OTHERS SAY YOU WERE A STRATEGIST

AN ACTIVIST

TO THE ENGLISH YOU WERE AN ANTAGONIST

YOU FOUGHT AND DEFEATED THE WICKED COLONIALIST

CONJURING UP YOUR AFRICAN CULTURE & SPIRITS

YOU WERE A SPIRITUALIST

FROM WEST AFRICA YOU CAME

MODERN-DAY GHANA, NOW IT'S NAMED

SPECIFICALLY, FROM THE AKAN PEOPLE

YOU WERE A GIANT, YOU WERE A STEEPLE

ADORED FOR YOUR COURAGE AND BRAVERY

YOU FOUGHT VALIANTLY AGAINST SLAVERY

LEADING PLATOONS OF MAROONS
YOU CREATED HAVOC ON THE BRITISH
BRUTAL RULE
TRAINED IN GUERILLA WARFARE
THE BRITISH ARTILLERY YOU DID NOT FEAR
URBAN LEGEND CLAIMED, YOU BLOCKED
BULLETS WITH YOUR DERRIERE
AS YOU FOUGHT, AS YOU COMMANDEERED
TODAY YOUR NAME IS RESPECTED AND REVERED
YOU GAVE US EMPOWERMENT
OUR EMBODIMENT OF RESILIENCE
TO THE OPPRESSORS AND THE OPPONENT
YOU WERE EVIL, YOU WERE AN OMEN
THE BRITISH BRANDED YOU AN ENEMY
YOU WERE TOUGH AND MENACING
YOU ARE, JAMAICA'S ONLY NATIONAL HEROINE
YOU AND YOUR POSSE FREED MANY OF THE ENSLAVED
THE ABENG WAS USED TO COMMUNICATE
YOUR HIDEOUT WAS THE BLUE MOUNTAIN ENCLAVES
TODAY, YOU ARE BURIED AT BUMP GRAVE

YOU ARE HONORED FOR YOUR LEGACY

YOUR PORTRAIT IS ON JAMAICA'S $500 CURRENCY

WE SALUTE YOU OUR ESTEEMED ASHANTI

SOMETIMES CALLED GRANNY NANNY

OUR BELOVED QUEEN NANNY

WHAT'S YOUR LEGACY?

WHAT'S YOUR CONTRIBUTION TO THIS EARTH?

WHAT'S YOUR LEGACY, WHAT'S YOUR WORTH?

WHAT ARE YOUR ACCOMPLISHMENTS?

WHAT'S YOUR STANCE ON IMPOVERISHMENT?

DID YOU GIVE AID, DID YOU ASSIST?

WERE YOU A PHILANTHROPIST?

WHAT DID YOU GIVE BACK TO THIS WORLD?

DID YOU, VOLUNTEER, DID YOU SERVE

DID YOU TRY TO EASE THE SUFFERINGS ON THE LAND?

DID YOU LEND A HELPING HAND?

DID YOU PROVIDE RELIEF TO THE UNDER-PRIVILEGE?

DID YOU EMBRACE THE SAYING? IT TAKES A VILLAGE

HOW DID YOU SPEND YOUR TIME ON THIS PLANET?

WERE YOU BENEVOLENT, WERE YOU CHARITABLE?

DID YOU UPLIFT THE FRAIL AND FALLIBLE?

DID YOU MENTOR TO THE DISADVANTAGE?

TO THE DESTITUTE DID YOU GIVE AN ADVANTAGE

WERE YOU A BENEFACTOR TO SCHOOLS?

DID YOU LIVE BY THE GOLDEN RULE?

DID YOU GIVE ASSISTANCE TO THE POOR?

DID YOU HELP SOMEONE RISE UP AND SOAR?

YOU MUST LEAVE YOUR MARK ON THIS EARTH

WITH POSITIVITY IN YOUR HEART, SHOW YOUR WORTH

FOR OTHERS GO THE EXTRA MILE

MAKE THEM FEEL SPECIAL AND WORTHWHILE

ADVOCATE FOR THE POOR AND MARGINALIZE

SHOW EMPATHY, RESPECT THE ELDERLY

SUPPORT YOUR COMMUNITY

GIVE THE YOUTHS A CHANCE, GIVE THEM OPPORTUNITIES

ERASE HATE, PROMOTE LOVE UNCONDITIONALLY

BE UNSELFISH, TREAT EVERYONE RESPECTFULLY

FROM YOUR MIND PURGE ENVY AND JEALOUSY

FORGIVE AND LOVE YOUR FELLOW HUMAN BEINGS

SHARE WITH OTHERS, PROJECT YOUR SYNERGY

THEN YOU CAN SAY, YOU LEFT YOUR MARK ON SOCIETY

"YOUR HISTORY, YOUR LEGACY"

She Is Your Mother

Sometimes she labored as a prostitute
Other times pushing a handcart
Peddling snacks and juice
Her upbringing was one rife with abuse
Nine rough months she carried you
With no help, no breakthrough
She fed, protected, and sheltered you
Your desires, you were able to pursue
As she supported and provided the revenue
Now, you are mortified and ashamed of her
Because she is a street entrepreneur
Nobody must know of her not yesterday
Now or tomorrow
All connections to her you avoid
Maintaining your secret is a joy
All memories with her are denied
Your friends she must not meet
With her you must not be seen

WHENEVER YOU PASS HER ON THE STREETS

YOU HIDE, YOU FLEE

SECRETLY, YOU WISHED SHE WAS DECEASED

CALLING HER, MA, MOTHER, OR MOM

YOU ABSTAIN

WITH HER YOU DID NOT WISH TO AFFILIATE

ACCEPT AND EMBRACE HER, DON'T TREAT HER WITH DISDAIN

DEMONSTRATE TO HER THAT YOU CARE

KEEP HER CLOSE, HOLD HER DEAR, SALUTE HER WITH ALL THE FANFARE

ADORE THIS WOMAN, FOR SHE IS YOUR MOTHER

SHOWER HER WITH LOVE AND GIVE HER ALL THE HONOR

THOUGHTS OF ABORTION

DON'T ABORT ME, I BEG YOU PLEASE

LISTEN TO MY HEARTBEAT

FEEL THE KICKS FROM MY TINY FEET

PAUSE YOUR THOUGHTS

WITH YOUR INTENTIONS DON'T PROCEED

I KNOW YOU DON'T KNOW ME YET

AND WE HAVE NOT OFFICIALLY MET

BUT I AM ADORABLE, YOUR HEART I WILL MELT

DON'T THROW ME AWAY, I AM NOT YOUR DOOMSDAY

I AM YOUR LOVE, I AM YOUR BABY

GIVE ME A CHANCE TO CELEBRATE MY BIRTHDAYS

DON'T TOSS ME DOWN THE TOILET

I AM NOT YOUR DEBT, DON'T BE STRESSED

I AM A BLESSINGS, I AM YOUR ASSET

NEITHER ABORT ME WITH THE DOCTOR'S AID

I KNOW YOU ARE AFRAID AND SCARED

BUT MOTHER DEAR, DON'T BE DISMAYED

BIRTH ME, GIVE ME UP FOR ADOPTION

DON'T DISCARD ME, YOU HAVE OTHER OPTIONS

I KNOW YOU HAVE DREAMS AND GREAT AMBITIONS

AND YOUR FUTURE IS UNCERTAIN

WITH FRUSTRATIONS

BUT LOVE ME, I AM YOUR CREATION

LEAVE ME BY THE FIRE STATION

OR LAY ME BY A HOUSE DOORSTEP

WHERE I CAN GET SOME HELP

I KNOW YOUR PREGNANCY IS UNPLANNED

AND YOU ARE SINGLE, WITH NO BOYFRIEND

NO MAN

IT ALSO SEEMS YOUR FUTURE IS CLUELESS

AND DAMMED

BUT MY MOTHER TO BE, GIVE ME A CHANCE TO BE A WOMAN OR MAN

I KNOW YOU RATHER BE WED, AND AFRAID OF WHAT LIES AHEAD

BUT IF YOU HAVE THE ABORTION, I AM GOING TO END UP DEAD

MY MOTHER, THINK TWICE ABOUT MY SLAUGHTER
I COULD BE YOUR SON OR YOUR DAUGHTER
I MIGHT GROW UP AND BECOME A NURSE
OR DOCTOR
PLEASE, MY MOTHER, GIVE ME A CHANCE
TO PROSPER
I PROMISE YOUR LIFE WILL NOT WITHER
AND I AM, HOPING
YOUR THOUGHTS OF ABORTING ME
YOU WILL RECONSIDER

A WOMAN'S CHOICE

I AM ONCE AGAIN PREGNANT

MY LIVING IS ROUGH, IT IS STAGNANT

I AM CONSIDERED WORTHLESS AND REPUGNANT

FAILURES IN MY LIFE IS APPARENT AND RAMPANT

THIS IS MY 6TH PREGNANCY; HOW CAN I AFFORD ANOTHER CHILD?

MY SITUATION IS DIRE, I AM DETESTED AND REVILED

I AM SORRY MY BABY BOY, I AM SORRY MY BABY GIRL

I KNOW MY DECISION IS NOT WISE, IT GONNA HURT

I OPTED TODAY, TO GET RID OF YOU, MY EMBRYO

I CANNOT COPE, I AM HEADING DOWN A SLOPE

I FEEL THERE IS NO HOPE, MY BACK IS AGAINST THE ROPE

MY CHILDREN, I AM UNABLE TO PROVIDE FOOD OR SHELTER

OVERALL, I AM NOT ABLE TO MAKE THEIR LIVES BETTER

I AM POOR, I FEEL DEFEATED, I AM A LOWLY BEGGAR

MEN I DEPEND ON AND SOMETIMES I GET HANDOUTS

WITH THEM, I EXCHANGE SEX FOR A PAYOUT

BY SOCIETY I AM TREATED AS UNEDUCATED AND A REJECT

I KNOW I SHOULD USE A CONDOM, I SHOULD PRACTICE SAFE SEX

SOME SAY A CONTRACEPTIVES I SHOULD SELECT

BUT MY SITUATION IS NOT SIMPLE, ITS VERY COMPLEX

THIS IS MY BODY AND I KNOW I HAVE RIGHTS

DO YOU UNDERSTAND MY DILEMMA OR MY PLIGHT?

WOULD YOU SAY MY CHOICE OF ABORTION IS JUSTIFIED?

Our Lives Matter

WE HAVE HELD UP OUR FIST FOR EONS

WE HAVE MARCHED FAR TOO LONG

SINGING HALLELUJAH AND WE CAN OVERCOME SONGS

WE DEMONSTRATE, BUSINESS BURNT

BUILDING TORN DOWN

NOW TAKING A KNEE IS OUR NEW PROTEST STANCE

MARTYRS ARE ELEVATED

NEW GRASS-ROOT LEADERS ARE BORN

FOR OVER 400 HUNDRED YEARS WE ARE WAITING

FOR OUR LIBERATION

BUT TODAY IS A NEW DAY, IT'S A NEW DAWN

IT'S A NEW REVOLUTION

WE ARE TIRED OF HEARING I CAN'T BREATHE

TIRED OF DEATH SENTENCES UPON US BEQUEATH

TIRED OF HEARING HANDS IN THE AIR

TIRED OF BEING SCARED, TIRED OF BEING ENSNARED

TIRED OF HEARING PLEASE DON'T SHOOT
TIRED OF THE POLICE BRUTE & PURSUITS
WHETHER WE SLEEP, EAT, WALK OR TALK
WHETHER WE DRIVE, JOG, RUN OR HAVE FUN
BIRD WATCHING AT THE PARK
ALL OF THE ABOVE ACTS WE ARE AT SOME FAULT
THE COPS ARE FREQUENTLY CALLED
AND WITH DEATH WE ARE EARMARKED
WE ARE ARRESTED, WE ARE BRUTALIZED
WE ARE REPRESSED, WE ARE DEHUMANIZED
WE ARE SILENCED, WE ARE CHASTISED
SOON WE ARE IN COFFINS, WE ARE THEN EULOGISED
EQUALITY AND JUSTICE, WE DEMAND
WE ARE NOT ANIMALS, WE ARE HUMAN
WE ARE TIRED OF THE PERSECUTION
PUT A STOP TO THE EXECUTION OF THE BLACK MAN
SUPPRESS THE KU KLUX KLAN
JUNE 19, 1865, THE LAST OF THE ENSLAVED
GAINED THEIR MANUMISSION

THEN CAME THE PEONAGE INSTITUTIONS

IT IS THE NEW SLAVERY, NOT A BETTER SOLUTION

NOW OUR EYES ARE OPEN

THE BLACK POPULACE HAVE SPOKEN

NO LONGER WE WILL BE BROKEN

WE WILL BE MIGHTY, WE WILL BE STRONG

WE WILL FORGE ON UNTIL WE REACH THE UPPER ECHELON

UNITED WE ARE, WE HAVE A NEW PROGRESSIVE VISION

COUNTING ON THIS GENERATION TO CARRY ON THE MISSION

AS WE TIRED OF THE SLAUGHTER OF OUR FATHERS

OUR MOTHERS, SONS, AND DAUGHTERS

RISE UP NEW LEADERS, WE SHALL EXPEL THE MARAUDERS

ACTION WE NEED, NOT TOO MUCH CHATTER

TIME IS NOW, NOT LATER, FOR OUR LIVES MATTER

Don't Cry For Me

DON'T WEEP FOR ME WHEN I DIE

YOU NEVER COMFORTED ME

WHEN I WAS SICK AND, IN MY PLIGHT

YOU NEVER SHOWED ME EMPATHY, WHEN I CRIED

NO VISITS FROM YOU, WHEN THINGS WERE AWRY

WHEN I NEEDED A FRIEND WHEN I NEEDED AN ALLY

YOU WERE NEVER AROUND, YOU WERE NEVER BY MY SIDE

I DON'T WANT YOU TO CRY FOR ME WHEN I DIE

I DON'T WANT YOUR EXCUSES, NOR YOUR ALIBIS

DON'T MAKE UP FIBS OR LIES, YOUR ABSENCE IS NOT JUSTIFIED

I THOUGHT UPON YOU I COULD COUNT

ON YOU, I COULD RELY

BELIEVED WE WERE A TEAM AND OUR FRIENDSHIP WAS TIGHT

NOW IT'S NIL, NOW IT'S VOID

SO PLEASE DON'T CRY, WHEN I AM GONE

WHEN I DIE

YOU PRETENDED WE WERE FRIENDS FOR LIFE
TOO LATE NOW, NO RECONCILIATION, BYE, BYE
MAYBE WE WILL BE FRIENDS AGAIN
AND REUNITE IN THE NEXT LIFETIME

You Are Not My Friend

I KNOW YOUR TYPE, I GOT A TASTE OF YOUR BITE

I FEEL YOUR STING, VENOM YOU BRING

YOU ARE SLY, YOU ARE WILD, YOUR ATTITUDE REVILED

YOU CAN'T BE TRUSTED, YOUR PERSONALITY IS DISGUSTING

YOU ARE A TRAITOR, A COLLABORATOR

YOU ROBBED ME OF MY SANITY & MY SWAGGER

YOU ARE A BACKSTABBER, AN ATTACKER

PLUNGING YOUR DAGGER, INTO MY WOUND

RESTRICTING MY ENERGY, CURBING MY MOOD

BEING AROUND YOU, I FEEL MY LIFE IS DOOMED

I KNOW YOU VERY WELL

YOUR SHADINESS I CAN READ, I CAN TELL

FROM YOU I WANT TO GET AWAY, I WANT TO SAY FAREWELL

MY LIFE YOU WANT TO MANEUVER

YOU ARE A USER

YOU ARE NOT GENUINE, YOU ARE NOT A FRIEND
BEING AROUND YOU, I CAN'T GET AHEAD
I CAN'T RISE, I CAN'T ASCEND
YOU ONLY COME AROUND ME, TO GET HAND OUT
YOU, DON'T CARE IF I AM IN FAMINE OR DROUGHT
YOU WERE NEVER FOR ME, YOUR ACTIONS
I LOATHE
MY FIRE YOU DOUSED, MY FLAME YOU BLOWOUT
YOU HAVE NO HEART, YOU HAVE NO SOUL
YOU STUNTED MY GROWTH AND BELITTLE MY GOALS
YOU ARE ONLY IN MY PRESENCE TO GRAB AND COLLECT
YOU ARE CONNIVING, MEETING YOU I REGRET
NO LOVE YOU GIVE, YOU STIFLE MY SPIRIT
THIS UNION I REFUSE TO SUBMIT
YOUR ACTIONS I CAN'T FORGET, I CAN'T FORGIVE
PLEASE EXIT MY LIFE, TO THIS FRIENDSHIP
I WON'T COMMIT

LAUGHTER

AN OLD PROVERB SAY

LAUGHTER IS THE BEST MEDICINE

ANY TIME OF THE DAY AND I MUST AGREE

LAUGHTER IMPLIES JOY, HAPPINESS, OR GLEE

LAUGHTER CAN BE SPONTANEOUS, OR IT CAN BE FORCED

LAUGHTER CAN BE A SNICKER OR AN OUTBURST

LAUGHTER CAN BE A CHUCKLE OR A GIGGLE

LAUGHTER CAN BE GENERATED WHEN TICKLED

LAUGHTER CAN BE SNORTY OR LOUD AS A ROAR

LAUGHTER CAN LEAVE YOU CONVULSING TO THE FLOOR

LAUGHER CAN BE GUTTURAL OR FROM DEEP DOWN IN THE BELLY

LAUGHTER IS LIKE SUNSHINE, BRIGHT

AND MERRY

LAUGHTER CAN BE HYSTERICAL LEAVING YOU

IN TEARS

SOMETIMES LAUGHTER IS HILARIOUS

YOU WILL GRIN FROM EAR TO EAR
WE SOMETIMES LAUGH WHEN SOMEONE FALL
OR BAWL
LAUGHTER CAN BE SO FUNNY LEAVING YOU
IN STITCHES
WE FREQUENTLY LAUGH AT A COMIC OR WHEN
A JOKE IS SILLY
LAUGHTER CAN BE SO HUMOROUS INDUCING ONE
TO PEE
LAUGHTER CAN BE RAUCOUS, INFECTIOUS
AND LIVELY
THERE ARE NO COMPARISONS
LAUGHTER IS INDEED THE BEST MEDICINE

NEVER AGAIN

DURING WORLD WAR 2, HITLER THE TYRANT RULED

WAR WAS WAGED, PROPAGANDA PREVAILED

THE GERMAN POSTULATED THEY WERE THE MASTER RACE

AMIDST ANTI-SEMITIC CAMPAIGNS, THE HORRIFIC NAZI REIGNED

THEY WERE EVIL, INHUMANE, AND CRUDE

THEY EXECUTED SIX MILLION JEWS

ALONG WITH MILLIONS OF GYPSIES, THE DISABLED AND HOMOSEXUALS

SLAVIC, LEFTIST, AND JEHOVAH WITNESS LIVES WERE ALSO DEPLETED

MENGELE EXPERIMENTED ON TWINS

AND THEM, HE MISTREATED

BABIES BORN, THEN DROWNED, DESPITE THE MOTHERS' PLEADING

MANY WERE ROBBED OF THEIR BUSINESS BELONGINGS, AND ABODE PLACED IN

CONCENTRATION CAMPS AND CONFINED TO GHETTOS

THE BRUTAL SECRET POLICE, WAS THE GESTAPO

THE NAZIS SUPPORTERS WERE COLLABORATORS

MILLIONS WAS LED TO THE GAS CHAMBERS AND INCINERATORS

THOUSANDS STARVED; THE DISABLED EUTHANIZED

BABIES, PREGNANT WOMEN, THE YOUNG

THE OLD, AND EVEN RABBIS

WERE SUFFOCATED AND DIED FROM ZYKLON B

AND CARBON MONOXIDE

THE RESISTANCE FIGHTERS WERE SYMPATHIZERS AND ALLIES

THE NAZIS, THEY TRIED TO DESTABILIZE

THE HOLOCAUST WAS DREADFUL, IT WAS A VIOLATION OF HUMAN LIFE

IT WAS MASS MURDER, A MASSACRE, IT WAS GENOCIDE

THE VITRIOLIC, THE PREJUDICE, AND THE HATE

THE FEAR THAT PERMEATED EUROPE'S AIR

THE ALMOST EXTERMINATION OF

THE JEWISH RACE

THIS ABOMINABLE AND DESPICABLE ACT MUST NEVER HAPPEN AGAIN

DOMESTIC ABUSE

I AM YOUR LOVER, I AM YOUR WIFE

YET YOU BATTER ME AND WANT TO TAKE MY LIFE

I AM DISABLED, TO CARE FOR MYSELF I AM UNABLE

YOU TAKE AWAY MY RIGHTS AND TREAT ME LIKE A PARASITE

I AM ELDERLY, FEEBLE, AND FRAIL

ENDLESSLY YOU MISTREAT ME, MAKING ME SCARED

I AM THAT CHILD YOU FREQUENTLY BEAT

CONSTANTLY BERATE AND REBUKE

ALL ARE ILLUSTRATIONS OF DOMESTIC ABUSE

PHYSICAL, SEXUAL, PSYCHOLOGICAL, AND ECONOMIC TOO

INTIMIDATION, MONEY MISMANAGEMENT

BEING KEPT UNSAFE AND WITHHOLDING FOOD

LEFT SOILED, UNKEMPT, AND TREATED UNCOUTH

ARE DOMESTIC ABUSE CASES TOO

DON'T TURN A BLIND EYE, DON'T ACT AS IF YOU ARE MUTE

IF YOU SEE MULTIPLE BRUISES, SKIN MARKED WITH BLACK & BLUE

BLACK EYES, BURNS, AND BEDWETTING

CEASE WITH THE ALIBIS, STOP THE EXCUSE

ALL LIVES ARE IMPORTANT, ALL LIVES ARE VALUED

REPORT DOMESTIC VIOLENCE, REPORT DOMESTIC ABUSE

OLD-TIME REGGAE

BRING BACK LOVE TO THE MUSIC

GO BACK TO THE BASICS

BRING BACK THE LYRICAL MASTERS

BIG UP THE POSITIVE SONG AUTHORS

BRING BACK DECENCY AND CONSCIOUSNESS

UPHOLD TRUTH AND RIGHTEOUSNESS

THIS MUSIC GENRE ONCE STOOD UP FOR THE POOR

SO, GO BACK TO THE CORE

WHEN MARLEY BROUGHT FAME, PETER TOSH HAD GAME

AND THE SMOOTHEST VOICE IN TOWN, BELONGED TO DENNIS BROWN

BUNNY WAILER HAS BEING HOLDING IT DOWN

BARRINGTON LEVY HAD THE MOST MELODIOUS SOUND

TOOTS AND THE MAYTALS, BLACK UHURU, BURNING SPEAR WERE PIONEERS

GREGORY ISAACS WAS COOL, IN THE PAST HALF PINT AND COCOA TEA RULED

NOW ON THE RISE, AND IN THE MIX IS THE
TALENTED CHRONIXX

ALONG WITH DAMIAN MARLEY, KABAKA, KOFFEE,
JESSE ROYAL, AND PROTÉGÉ

LOVE AND POSITIVITY IS ALWAYS PORTRAYED

I AM TALKING ABOUT OUR SWEET REGGAE MUSIC

WHICH IS RASTA INFLUENCED AND ECLECTIC

INGRAINED IN JAMAICA'S MUSICAL CULTURE
SINCE THE 1960S

FOCUS ON SOCIAL ISSUES AND WITH CONSCIOUS
LYRICS

IRIE, SOOTHING AND THERAPEUTIC

SO, LET'S ERADICATE FROM THE MUSIC

THE NEGATIVITY, VIOLENCE, AND THE GORE

REINSTATE THIS MELODIOUS GRANDEUR

AND ONCE AGAIN MAKE OUR JAMAICAN
TREASURE SOAR

SAGGING PANTS

YOUNG MAN PULL UP YOUR PANTS, IT DRAGS

IT SAGS, YOU LOOK LIKE A SCUMBAG

BE MODEST, BE DISCREET

MAKE YOUR APPEARANCE CLEAN, BE NEAT

YOU LOOK IS UNTIDY, YOUR LOOK IS OBSCENE

YOUNG MEN PULL UP YOUR PANTS

LOOK SPICK AND SPAN

WEAR A BELT, DRAW YOUR SLACKS UP TO YOUR WAIST

A RESPECTABLE IMAGE YOU MUST PORTRAY

YOU CALL YOUR SAGGING PANTS STYLE? DRESS WITH DECENCY, AND PRIDE

DON'T WANT TO SEE YOUR BUM, BUTTOCKS, OR BEHIND

DON'T WANT TO SEE THE HOLES, THE TEAR IN YOUR UNDERWEAR

PLEASE, HIDE YOUR DERRIERE, DRESS WITH FLAIR

THE HISTORY AND TREND OF SAGGING PANTS BEGAN IN PRISONS

IT SHOULDN'T BE EMULATED, IT SHOULD BE FORBIDDEN

INMATES WORE THEIR PANTS WITHOUT BELTS, AS A SUICIDE PRECAUTION

IT IS AN OUTRAGE, TO SEE THE LONGEVITY OF THIS SO-CALLED FASHION

FOR THIS CRAZE WE HAVE NO ADORATION, NO PASSION

THIS STYLE WE JUST CAN'T FATHOM

AGAIN, WE DON'T WISH TO SEE YOUR CRACKS

AND YOUR BOTTOMS

THIS FAD MUST GO AWAY, IT MUST BE ABANDONED

ODE TO POLITRICKS

MR POLITICIAN PLEASE

NO MORE ECONOMIC SQUEEZE

WE ARE TIRED OF YOUR GAME, YOUR RHETORIC IS LAME

WE WANT SOME OF THE WEALTH, WE REQUIRE GOOD HEALTH

WE AT THE BOTTOM OF THE TOTEM, DON'T WANT HANDOUTS OR TOKENS

WE WANT WHAT'S OURS, NOT WHAT'S YOURS

WE WANT A PIECE OF THE PIE, SO, OUR CHILDREN WON'T DIE

INCREASE THE MINIMUM WAGE, ITS AN OUTRAGE

LOOK AT THE PITTANCE WE ARE PAID

UP THE LADDER WE WANT TO CLIMB

NOT HELD DOWN AT ALL THE TIME

INSTITUTE FAIR HOUSING GUIDELINES

NOT IN GHETTOS CONFINED

WE WANT A CHANCE TO STAY ALIVE

NOT STRUGGLE, BUT THRIVE

HOW DO YOU SLEEP, WHILE THE MASSES

WAIL AND WEEP?

LIVING LAVISHLY, WITH YOUR ABUNDANT DRINKS AND FEAST

WHILE MANY HAVE NO FOOD TO EAT

YOU ROB FROM THE POOR, THEN YOU APPEAR AT THEIR DOORS

SEEKING THEIR SUPPORT, BEGGING FOR THEIR VOTES

WHEN IT IS ELECTION TIME

YOU MAKE FALSE PROMISES, HARSH POLICIES

TRAMPLING THE LITTLE MAN

ENRICHING THE BIG MAN

WE WILL NO LONGER BOW, WE WILL DISAVOW

YOUR DEMANDS AND COMMANDS, DO YOU UNDERSTAND?

SO, MR POLITICIAN, PLEASE

NO MORE DECEIT, NO MORE OF YOUR TRICKERY DISEASE

NEXT ELECTION TIME WE KNOW OUR VOTES

YOU WILL SEEK

BUT YOU, AND YOUR POLITICAL PARTY

FROM OUR MINDS WE WILL DELETE

BLACK WOMEN

BLACK WOMEN KNOW YOUR WORTH

YOU ARE QUEENS, MOTHERS OF THE EARTH

TEACH YOUR KIDS GOOD MORAL VALUES

ONES THEY CAN ASPIRE TO

BLACK WOMEN YOUR FAMILIES ARE IN CRISIS

IMPLEMENT RULES, BE DECISIVE

BE ROLE MODELS, STOP BEING MINDLESS

FOR YOU ARE PRECIOUS, YOU ARE PRICELESS

BLACK WOMEN, IT'S NOT ALL ABOUT, TWERKING

FALSE HAIR, FALSE EYELASHES, GUCCI

AND BIRKINS

GET A CAREER, GET AN EDUCATION

SET A POSITIVE FOUNDATION

LET THEM CALL YOU BY YOUR NAME

YOUR EMPRESS TITLE RECLAIM

BLACK WOMEN SET STANDARDS TO EMULATE

REJECT MEN WHO USE YOU ONLY TO PROCREATE

LOVE YOURSELF, DON'T BE PLACED ON A SHELF

DO SOME INTROSPECT, DEMAND RESPECT

YOU ARE LIKE FINE WINE, WHY ARE YOU NOT CONSIDERED WIVES

YOU ARE RELEGATED TO SIDE CHICKS

AND CONCUBINES

AVOID MEN WHO ARE ENAMORED ONLY BY YOUR

LIPS, HIPS, AND BOOTY

LET THEM KNOW YOU CAN THINK

YOU HAVE BRAINS

AND NOT JUST YOUR OUTER BEAUTY

LET THEM RESPECT YOU, FOR YOU ARE WORTHY

YOU ARE DIGNIFIED, AVOIDING BULL-SHIT

AND CONTROVERSIES

ALLOW YOUR WOMAN-POWER TO SHINE

LET THEM HONOR, SHOW RESPECT TO YOU

AT ALL TIMES

BECAUSE YOU ARE BLACK, YOU ARE QUEEN

YOU ARE DIVINE

OUR HAIRSTYLES

BLACK HAIRSTYLES ARE VERSATILE

FROM BALDHEAD TO AFRO

DREADLOCKS TO CORNROWS

THAT'S HOW WE ROCK, THAT'S HOW WE FLOW

FROM WIGS TO CURLS, WEAVES TO PERMS

NATURAL HAIR STAND FIRM

FROM GRAY TO DYED CROWN, THAT'S HOW WE GET DOWN

SMOOTH AND STRAIGHT

SHORT WITH A PIXIE CUT

NO IFS OR BUTS, THAT'S HOW WE STRUT

PONYTAIL AND SHORT BOB, BUNS, AND BANGS

OUR HAIR DOS' ALWAYS LOOK GLAM

WHETHER MULTI-COLORED, BLEACHED

BRAIDS OR BANTU KNOTS

OUR HAIRSTYLES IS A HIT ON THE SPOT

OUR HAIR IS OUR PRIDE

IT DEFINES OUR PROFILE, ADMIRED AND COPIED ALL THE TIME

THE BLACK WOMAN UNIQUE STYLE

FOR BLACK FATHERS

BLACK FATHERS

SUPPORT YOUR WIVES AND BABY MOTHERS

THEY HAVE BEEN WAITING ON YOU FOR A WHILE

THEY NEED YOUR SUPPORT AT ALL TIMES

DESIST FROM YOUR SELF EXILE

BE A PARENT, FOSTER YOUR CHILDREN'S DEVELOPMENT

BE A POSITIVE VOICE, GIVE THEM UPLIFTMENT

SO MANY OF OUR YOUTHS, BOYS SPECIFICALLY BUT GIRLS TOO

NO MALE ROLE MODELS THEY CAN PURSUE

THEY HAVE NO ONE TO LOOK TO

THEY NEED YOUR ASSURANCE; THEY NEED TO FEEL VALUED

YOUR ABSENTEEISM IS DISTURBING THE MISSION

CAUSING OUR MALES TO BE PLACED IN JAILS AND PRISONS

BRING ABOUT A NEW VISION, IMPROVE THEIR LIVING CONDITIONS

WE NEED TO RAISE DISTINGUISHED MEN

GIVE THEM A FUTURE, AND NOT A DEAD-END

GUIDE THEM, ON WAYS TO BE A MAN

TEACH THEM TO RESPECT WOMEN

OUR BLACK BOYS AND GIRLS NEED LOVE

AND HUGS

NOT GANGS, GUN, OR DRUGS, NOT TO BE LABELED AS THUGS

EDUCATE THEM ON LIFE LESSONS, IN THEIR LIVES BE A BLESSING

ENCOURAGE THEM TO STAY IN SCHOOL, TO BE LEADERS AND NOT FOOLS

BLACK FATHERS, IT'S TIME TO STEP UP AND

FILL THE VOID

SHOW UP, BE PRESENT, DON'T JUST BE A

SPERM DONOR, DON'T HIDE

BE A MAN, BE A FATHER, LIVE UPRIGHT

BUILD BLACK FAMILIES, BUILD BLACK CHILDREN LIVES

THE DECEIVER

YOU ARE A FAKE, YOU ARE A SHAM

A FRAUD, I AM TIRED OF YOUR SCAM

YOU WERE MY HUSBAND, YOU WERE MY MAN

BUT YOU PLAYED ME AND LEFT ME IN A JAM

I TOILED HARD WHILE YOU ATTENDED SCHOOL

NOW YOU ARE A PROFESSIONAL, YOU THINK OF ME AS A FOOL

I NO LONGER FIT YOUR PROFILE, I AM OFTEN RIDICULED

YOU ARE AN IMPOSTOR, YOU ARE A CHEAT

A DECEIVER, YOU ARE DEAD TO ME

TIRED OF THIS RELATIONSHIP, JUST WANT TO BE FREE

IT WAS SUPPOSED TO BE TWO OF US

AND NOT THREE

WE WERE IN A PARTNERSHIP, WE WERE A TEAM

TO YOUR MISTRESS YOU WERE COMMITTED

AND CERTAINLY NOT TO ME

SO, I AM OUT OF HERE, I HAVE TO GET OUT

I MUST FLEE

20 YEARS I HAVE INVESTED, 20 YEARS WE BOTH HAD DREAM

MARRIAGE, CHILDREN, A BIG HOUSE

AND ONE FAMILY

NOW, YOU HAVE MOVED ON TO ANOTHER

YOU SAID SHE IS "PRETTIER, SEXIER, AND YOUNGER" THAN ME

YOU BLAMED IT ON MID-LIFE CRISIS, YOUR DESIRES, AND VICES

NEVER KNEW I WOULD BE LABELED A DIVORCEE

ALWAYS WANTED MY CHILDREN'S DAD TO BE PRESENT, NOT AN ABSENTEE

I STRIVED FOR A TWO-PARENT HOUSEHOLD WITH LOVE AND STABILITY

BUT MY WISH WAS NOT GRANTED, THERE WERE NO GUARANTEES

YOU DESTROYED OUR FAMILY UNIT, YOU DEMOLISHED OUR LEGACY

BUT THAT'S LIFE, IT'S MY STORY, MY REALITY

WOMEN'S DAY

INTERNATIONAL WOMEN'S DAY

COMMEMORATED ANNUALLY ON MARCH 8TH

TO MEMORIALIZE THE ACHIEVEMENTS THAT WE'VE MADE

GET OUR BIG UPS, RECOGNITION

AND ACCOLADES

WE ARE OFTEN OVERLOOKED, WITHOUT AWARDS AND PRAISE

GENDER EQUALITY WE DEMAND, AND WHAT WE SAY

OVERALL PARITY WE COMMAND, THIS SHOULDN'T BE A DEBATE

THE FOLLOWING CRITERIA SOCIETY SHOULD STIPULATE

FEMALE GENITAL MUTILATIONS WE MUST ELIMINATE

VIOLENCE AGAINST WOMEN WE SHOULD OBLITERATE

THERE SHOULD BE A MANDATE

ALL GIRLS MUST BE SCHOOLED, WE MUST EDUCATE

FOR WE ARE WORLD LEADERS, SENATORS
AND PRIME MINISTERS
LAWYERS, AND RELIGIOUS PREACHERS
BUSINESS OWNERS AND TEACHERS
POLICE, ATHLETES, AND ACADEMICS WITH DEGREES
OTHER PROFESSIONALS WITH PH.D.'S
WE ARE DOCTORS, NURSES WE ARE ENGINEERS
WE ARE TRAILBLAZERS, WE ARE PIONEERS
WE ARE WIVES, WE ARE DAUGHTERS
WE ARE SISTERS
WE ARE BEARERS OF CHILDREN
WE ARE COURAGEOUS, WE ARE AMBITIOUS
WE ARE DRIVEN
WE ARE FEMALES, WE ARE GIRLS, WE ARE WOMEN

Watered Down Rasta

HAS RASTA BEEN DILUTED?
WHERE ARE THOSE WHO FOUGHT
AGAINST THE BABYLON SYSTEM?
WHERE ARE THOSE DEFENDING PAN-AFRICANISM?
WHERE ARE THOSE WHO FOUGHT AGAINST THE
OPPRESSORS AND SUPPRESSORS
WHERE ARE THE BLACK LIBERATORS?
WHERE ARE THE FACILITATORS?
WHAT HAPPENED TO THE CALL?
AND THE CHANT OF BACK TO AFRICA?
WHERE ARE THE TRUE RASTAS?
THE HOPE AND ASPIRATIONS FOR PEOPLE IN
THE BLACK DIASPORA
WHERE IS THE FIGHT FOR AND
THE MOVEMENT OF BACK TO AFRICA?
NOW, WE HAVE THE CHILDREN OF OUR COLONIAL
MASTERS
LEADING THE RASTA ORDER
IGNORING THE MANIFESTO OF SELASSIE

LEONARD HOWELL, MARCUS GARVEY
AND THE LYRICS OF TOSH AND MARLEY
HOW CAN WE ALLOW INFILTRATIONS OF OUR CULTURE?
ALLOWING IT TO BE SEPULTURED?
RASTA LOCKS NOW A FASHION STATEMENT
NYABINGHI, BOBO LIVING NOW IN ABATEMENT
RASTA BEING IS REAL CONSCIOUSNESS AND NOT FOR ENTERTAINMENT
VOCALIZED REPARATION AS SLAVERY'S REPAYMENT
GET RID OF COMMERCIAL DREADS
DISPLAY THE REAL THOROUGHBRED
RASTA, DREAD NATTY DREAD
LET'S EVOKE THE SPIRIT AND CALL FOR BLACK POWER
NEVER FORGET THE ATROCITIES AGAINST MAMA AFRICA
LET'S CONTINUE OUR BLACK PHILOSOPHY
LET'S BRING BACK VALUE TO RASTA SOCIETY

INSPIRED BY CONVERSATION ON THE CUTTING EDGE BY MUTABURUKA

You Are a Vanguard

YOU ARE YOUR OWN BOSS; YOU BEAR YOUR OWN CROSS

TO THE BEAT OF YOUR DRUM, YOU MARCH

AHEAD YOU FORGE, NO MATTER THE COST

ASSERTIVE YOU ARE, YOU DON'T FUSS

YOU DON'T SPAR

YOU ARE DETERMINED, YOU ARE FOCUSED

YOU AIM FOR THE STAR

SOMETIMES YOU FAIL, SOMETIMES YOU FALL

YOU DON'T WALLOW IN SELF PITY

RARELY YOU BAWL

UP YOU WILL RISE AND STAND TALL

YOU ARE READY FOR THE CHALLENGES, EVEN IF YOU HAVE TO CRAWL

YOU ARE PREPARED TO BREAK DOWN THE BARRIERS

AND PENETRATE THE WALLS

LIFE IS NOT EASY, YES, IT IS SOMETIMES HARD

BUT DIFFICULTIES YOU WILL OVERCOME

BECAUSE GOD IS YOUR GUIDE AND YOUR GUARD

PHYSICALLY AND MENTALLY FIT YOU ARE

PLEASE DON'T GIVE UP, DON'T WITHDRAW

WITH PATIENCE, AND AMBITION, MAINTAIN YOUR STANDARDS

BE STEADFAST IN YOUR JOURNEY, AIM FOR THE LONG HAUL

YOU ARE RELENTLESS, YOU ARE A VANGUARD

What Are Your Intentions?

WHAT ARE YOUR PLANS, WHAT ARE YOUR INTENTIONS?

YOU SAY YOU WANT ME, YOU WANT TO BE MY MAN

AM I HEARING CORRECTLY OR I AM HEARING WRONG?

I WANT TO KNOW YOUR EXPECTATIONS

WE NEED TO HAVE A CONVERSATION

GO AHEAD SUBMIT YOUR APPLICATION

THIS IS WHAT I THINK, LET ME STATE MY OPINION

I KNOW YOU WANT ME, YOU WANT TO BE MY MAN

BUT YOU MUST HAVE A PLAN, TELL ME YOUR INTENTIONS

FIRST IT WILL BE MARRIAGE, ASKING FOR MY HAND

THEN I BECOME YOUR WIFE, YOU BECOME MY HUSBAND

A HOME WE WILL HAVE, WITH TWO PARENTS NOT ONE

WE WILL BE A UNIT, A FAMILY, TOGETHER WE WILL BOND

ME, YOU, OUR DAUGHTER, AND OUR SON

SO I ASK AGAIN, WHAT ARE YOUR INTENTIONS?

IF YOU AGREE WITH MY POSITION, I HAVE CERTAIN PRE-CONDITIONS

WE WILL BE PROVIDERS, WE WILL BOTH BRING IN PROVISIONS

WE WILL BE IN THIS RELATIONSHIP FOR THE LONG RUN

WE WILL SUPPORT EACH OTHER

NO CONTRADICTIONS

THERE WILL BE DISAGREEMENTS, BUT ARGUMENTS WE WON'T PROLONG

OUR LOVE WILL BE BETWEEN US BOTH, NO OTHER WOMAN OR MAN

WE WILL BOTH BE PARENTS, NO ABSENTEE FATHER, NOR SEPARATION

THAT'S MY DESIRE, THOSE ARE MY CONDITIONS

SO HOLLER AT ME, IF YOU AGREE WITH MY PROPOSITION

DO YOU HAVE ANY QUESTIONS, I AM OPEN TO NEGOTIATIONS

LET ME KNOW, WHAT ARE YOUR INTENTIONS?

I THANK YOU, LORD

I THANK YOU, LORD, EACH AND EVERY DAY

IN THE MORNING, NOONTIME, OR AT THE END OF THE DAY

TO YOU I ALWAYS PRAY

WHETHER SUNSHINE, CLOUDY OR RAINY DAYS

YOUR NAME IS WORTHY TO BE PRAISE

I THANK YOU FOR YOUR BENEVOLENCE

I THANK YOU FOR YOUR MERCIES

AND I THANK YOU FOR YOUR GRACE

I THANK YOU, LORD, THAT MY SINS YOU FORGAVE

I THANK YOU, LORD, IN YOUR NAME I AM SAVED

FROM YOU I WILL NEVER STRAY

YOUR COMMANDMENTS I WILL ALWAYS OBEY

LORD YOU ARE ALWAYS WITH ME EVERY STEP OF THE WAY

ABOVE YOU LORD, NO ONE IS GREATER

FOR YOU ARE MY MAKER, THE CREATOR

FOREVER I WILL WORSHIP AND HONOR YOU

MY SAVIOR

My Melanin

I LOVE MY SKIN

MY BEAUTIFUL MELANIN

NO NEED TO BLEACH

MY MELANIN IS LIKE A PEACH

LUCIOUS AND SWEET

I LOVE MY SKIN

MY FLAWLESS MELANIN

RICH, DARK CHOCOLATE, AND SMOOTH

BLESSED WITH THIS SKIN SINCE BIRTH

SINCE YOUTH

NOW THAT'S THE TRUTH

I LOVE MY BEAUTIFUL SKIN

MY SUN-KISSED MELANIN

I WAS CREATED THIS WAY

GOD MADE NO MISTAKE

I LOVE MY ATTRACTIVE SKIN

I AM PROUD AND WEAR IT WITH A GRIN

MY LOVELY MELANIN

SOME HATE AND DISCRIMINATE

OTHERS TRY TO SEGREGATE

MANY WANT TO DISASSOCIATE

WITH MY BLACK SKIN

MY PRECIOUS MELANIN

BUT THE HATERS I WILL IGNORE

I WILL SAY IT ONCE MORE

I PROUDLY ADORE

MY GORGEOUS SKIN

MY TREASURED MELANIN

*L*ET PEACE REIGN

WHY THE DIVISION, WHY THE WAR

WHY THE INFIGHTS AND THE CONSTANT SPARS

WHY DO WE HAVE GANGS?

WHY TRIBES AND CLANS?

CAN'T WE ALL JUST GET ALONG

WHY THE CONFLICT, WHY THE ANGER

WHY THE HATE

WHY EACH OTHER'S CIVIL RIGHTS, WE MUST VIOLATE?

WHY THE DISTRESS, WHY THE CONTEMPT

WHY SUCCESS TO EACH OTHER WE PREVENT

WHY THE ENVY AND DISDAIN

WHY THE SCORN, WHY INFLICT PAIN

WHY NOT LET UNITY MANIFEST

WHY NOT CORDIALLY CONVERSE

SPREAD HARMONY THROUGH THE UNIVERSE

WHY DON'T WE DISPLAY LOVE, HATRED IS A DISEASE?

WHY NOT HAVE TREATIES, AND MAINTAIN PEACE

WHY NOT END ALL COMBATS

LET ALL HOSTILITIES CEASE

No Love For You

I USED TO LOVE YOU, BUT NOW I DON'T
YOU WANTED ME TO COME BACK TO YOU
BUT NO, I WON'T
DAILY WE FIGHT AND ENGAGED IN PHYSICAL BOUTS
TOO MUCH DRAMA, HAD TO CLOCK OUT
TOO MUCH FUSSING, WE HARDLY SPEAK
WE COULDN'T FREELY EXPRESS WHAT WE MEAN
WE COULDN'T CONVERSE, WE FREQUENTLY CURSE
WE GOT ON EACH OTHER NERVES
WE SCREAMED AND WE SHOUT
WE HAD TO TAKE A BREAK, IT WAS NECESSARY
TO CHECKOUT
I CARED FOR YOU, AND THERE WAS NEVER
ANY DOUBTS
RIGHT NOW, OUR RELATIONSHIP HAS DIED
IT IS HEADING SOUTH
OUR LOVE HAS CEASED GROWING, WE ARE IN A
DROUGHT
BUT HONESTLY, OUR LOVE IS JUST NOT VIABLE
IT NO LONGER HAS CLOUT
I USED TO LOVE YOU, BUT NOW I DON'T

My Disability

NO, I AM NOT LAZY

I AM JUST TEMPORARILY DISABLED

I MAY BE OUT OF COMMISSION FOR AWHILE

BUT SOON I HOPE TO REGAIN AND RECAPTURE

MY PREVIOUS LIFESTYLE

THROUGH FAITH AND PRAYER

I AM CONFIDENT I WILL RECOVER

I KNOW, I WILL BE STRONG ONCE AGAIN

BACK TO NORMAL, RID OF THIS STAIN

SO, DON'T TELL ME

TO SELL OR WORK ONLINE

FOR MY BODY TO MEND, IT WILL TAKE SOME TIME

PARKINSON'S DISEASE IS NOT A JOKE

IT'S LIKE I HAD A STROKE

PHYSICALLY I MUST

RECOUP AND RECUPERATE

AND MENTALLY RENEW AND REGENERATE

NO, I AM NOT LAZY

I AM JUST TEMPORARILY DISABLED
I HAVE WORKED SINCE MY TEEN
SO, I HAVE PRIDE AND SELF ESTEEM
I MIGHT HAVE TREMORS AND MY GAIT
IS UNSTEADY
BUT A MIRACLE IS COMING
AND I WILL BE WAITING AND I WILL BE READY
TO COMPLETE THIS ARDUOUS JOURNEY
BUT I BELIEVE BY GOD'S GRACE AND MERCY
ONCE AGAIN, I WILL BE HEALTHY AND STURDY

Thank You

TWO SIMPLE WORDS, EIGHT LETTERS
YET SOME OF US, FIND IT SO HARD TO UTTER
I AM FLABBERGASTED AND OFTEN DISMAYED
WHY THESE SIMPLE WORDS ARE HARD TO SAY?
WHENEVER YOU ARE PROVIDED A SERVICE
AND IF YOU RECEIVE A GIFT, GIVEN ASSISTANCE
SAY "THANK YOU" WITH LOVE AND CONVICTION
COMPLIMENTS GIVEN ON A JOB WELL DONE
GETTING ADVICE, COMFORTED WHEN SAD
OR SOMEONE DIES
BE APPRECIATIVE, THE WORDS "THANK YOU" VOCALIZE
MAKE YOUR GRACIOUSNESS KNOWN FROM THE START
GENUINELY SAY "THANK YOU" FROM THE HEART
WHEN KINDNESS IS RENDERED
IN WHATEVER FORM
DISPLAY YOUR APPRECIATION AND GRATITUDE
IN A MELLOW MOOD, SMILE AND SAY "THANK YOU"

You Are an Inspiration

YOU ARE A PHENOMENON

AN INSPIRATION

YOU ARE IN FOR THE LONG RUN, THE MARATHON

THE PAST IS GONE, TO THE FUTURE YOU MOVE ON

YOU ARE CONFIDENT OF A NEW VISION

YOU AIM TO ASCEND TO THE UPPER ECHELON

YOU ARE NOT IN FOR THE SHORT SPRINT

YOU REFUSED TO QUIT, NEGATIVE THOUGHTS YOU FORBID

WITH CONVICTION YOU PROCEED, KNOWLEDGE YOU SPEAK

THEY WON'T SEE YOU WEEP, YOU WALK

YOU DON'T CREEP

WISDOM YOU PREACH, IT IS PROJECTED IN YOUR SPEECH

YOU STRIVE TO PREVAIL, YOU EMPOWER OTHER FEMALES

DESPITE YOUR TRAVAILS, AND THE OBSTACLES IN YOUR WAY

YOU ARE AN EXAMPLE TO FOLLOW, UNITY IS YOUR MOTTO

YOU ARE A SHINING LIGHT, YOU DON'T GOSSIP OR BACKBITE

YOU SHOW GOODWILL, LOVE, AND POSITIVE VIBES

WHEN OTHERS ARE ASLEEP, YOU ARE WORKING HARD TO DEFEAT

THE NEGATIVITY AND ACHIEVE A HIGHER EDUCATIONAL DEGREE

YOU ARE WILLING TO LEARN, YOU ARE LIVING TO EARN

TO THE PAST YOU WON'T RETURN, UNITY YOU YEARN

Is Reconciliation Possible?

YOU SAY YOU LOVE ME

YET YOU TREAT ME SO BAD

YOU SAY YOU WON'T' LEAVE ME

BUT ANOTHER LOVER YOU HAVE

I AM CONFUSED, I AM SAD

I AM PUZZLED, I AM MAD

I THOUGHT OUR BOND WAS IRONCLAD

I DON'T KNOW WHERE WE ARE HEADED

NEVER KNEW THIS LOVE WOULD HAVE ENDED

THIS IS SO UNEXPECTED, I AM LOST, I FEEL DEJECTED

I THOUGHT EACH OTHER WE RESPECTED

MAYBE WE CAN MEET, MAYBE TONIGHT?

HAVE A DISCUSSION, AND SET THINGS RIGHT

FIX WHAT WE HAD AND ONCE AGAIN REUNITE

REKINDLE OUR RELATIONSHIP, AND MAYBE WE WILL RECONCILE

DON'T TELL US TO SHUT UP

DON'T TELL US TO SHUT UP AND STOP THE COMPLAINTS

YOU DON'T KNOW WHAT WE HAVE BEEN THROUGH

YOU DON'T KNOW OUR PAIN

WE HAVE BEEN BEATEN, RAPED, AND KILLED

BERATED BECAUSE OF THE COLOR OF OUR SKIN

LYNCHED, AMPUTATED, AND WHIPPED

OUR LIBERTY GONE, OUR FREEDOM CONSTRICT

YOU SAY, WE AREN'T HUMAN, ANIMALS WE DEPICT

FREE LABOR WE GAVE, YOUR COTTON WE PICKED

FROM SLAVERY TO THE ERA OF JIM CROW

WE TEND TO YOUR HOMES, YOUR FIELDS WE PLOUGHED

NOW WE ARE "LAZY" AND "NO GOOD NEGROES"

SO, DON'T TELL US TO SHUT UP AND STOP THE COMPLAINTS

INDICATING, WE ARE LUCKY TO LIVE IN THE GREAT UNITED STATES

YOU SAY, WE ARE FREED AND NO LONGER RESTRAINED

WE SHOULD BE GRATEFUL, WE ARE NOT ENSLAVED

OUR BLACK RACE, YOU PERSECUTE

YOU DISCRIMINATE

BECAUSE OF YOUR INBORN HATE

NO, WE WON'T SHUT UP, WE WILL CONTINUE TO COMPLAIN

WHAT IS FREE TO YOU, LIVING IN A POLICE STATE?

AND NO LONGER PICKING YOUR COTTON OR HARVESTING YOUR SUGAR CANE?

GIVEN THREE MEALS A DAY, IN YOUR PRISONS AND YOUR JAILS?

NO, WE WON'T SHUT UP AND STOP THE COMPLAINTS

FOR JUSTICE WE WILL FIGHT, FOR RACIAL EQUALITY WE'LL CAMPAIGN

UNTIL WE ALL ARE ON THE SAME LEVEL, AND WE ARE TREATED HUMANE

We Are Weary

AMERICA WE ARE CRYING

OUR PEOPLE ARE DYING

MOTHERS ARE WAILING

FATHERS ARE ACHING

OUR HEARTS ARE BLEEDING

OUR SOULS ARE PLEADING

OUR FAMILIES ARE WEEPING

ON THE STREETS OUR BLOOD SEEPING

THIS IS MODERN-DAY LYNCHING

IT'S CONVINCING

THEIR FALSE REPORTS ARE CONFLICTING

NO QUESTIONS ASKED, THEY REFUSED TO LISTEN

WITH GUNS DRAWN, THEY COME KILLING

IN THE PAST HANGING WAS THEIR AMMUNITION

DECIMATE THE BLACK AND BROWN SKINS

IS THEIR MISSION

SO MANY SIMILARITIES, TOO MANY REPETITION

DESPITE THE MARCH AND DEMONSTRATIONS

WE DON'T GET ANY ADJUDICATION

SLAY THEM ALL, BOY, GIRL, MAN, OR WOMAN

THERE ARE NO DIFFERENTIATION

SLAUGHTER ALL OF THE NEGRO NATION

THEY SAY IN AMERICA, "WE WANT ONLY CAUCASIAN"

IS IT A PLANNED ANNIHILATION, OF THE BLACK NATION?

I WANT AN EXPLANATION

CAN YOU EXPLAIN, I WANT TO UNDERSTAND?

TELL ME, HOW DID YOU ATTAIN SO MANY ACRES OF LAND?

I AM TALKING TO YOU, MR. EUROPEAN

WHILE THE ORIGINAL INHABITANTS, THE NATIVE AMERICANS

ARE CONFINED ON RESERVATIONS

THE AFRICANS SLAVED, AND THE FIELDS THEY MANNED

WITHOUT PAY, NO COMPENSATION

THEY WERE PROMISED A MULE AND FORTY ACRES OF LAND

UPON FREEDOM, UPON THEIR MANUMISSION

BUT PROMISES WAS NOT KEPT

THEY DID NOT RECEIVE NEITHER MULE NOR LAND

SO, GIVE US LAND, NOW THAT WILL BE OUR REPARATIONS

HOW CAN THE CROWN OWN 1/6 OF EARTH'S LAND?

IN CANADA, THE UK, AUSTRALIA, ASIA

AFRICA AND THE CARIBBEAN

THE QUEEN IS LISTED AS THE RICHEST "LEGAL" OWNER OF LAND

HOW CAN COLUMBUS DISCOVER COUNTRIES AND ISLANDS?

AND CLAIMED THEM IN THE NAME OF QUEEN ISABELLA AND KING FERDINAND

WHEN THOSE PLACES WERE ALREADY INHABITED BY PEOPLE ON THE LAND

THE INDIGENOUS, ABORIGINES OR THE AMERINDIANS

ON GOD'S FREE EARTH, HOW IS IT SOME PEOPLE OWN SO MANY ACRES OF LAND?

WHY THE POOR AND WORKING-CLASS, CAN'T AFFORD A PLOT OF LAND?

WHY ACQUIRING LAND, COST THOUSANDS AND MILLIONS?

THERE ARE HOMELESS FAMILIES, WOMEN, AND MEN, WHO ARE BANNED

FOR OCCUPYING VACANT LAND, SOME MAY CALL IT CAPTURED LAND

FROM THESE LAND THEY ARE OFTEN EJECTED WITH FORCED EVACUATION

LET'S MANDATE LAND REDISTRIBUTION

I ASKED AGAIN, WHY THE CROWN OWN SO MANY ACRES OF LAND?

I WANT TO KNOW, I WANT AN EXPLANATION

AM

I AM A FIGHTER, I AM A SURVIVOR

I HAVE BEEN THROUGH HELL, THROUGH THE FIRE

I AM A WINNER, I AM A VICTOR

I AM NOT A LOSER, NOT A QUITTER

I AM A TRAILBLAZER

I AM A TEAM PLAYER

I AM NOT A NAYSAYER, I DISLIKE FAILURES

I AM A WOMAN, I AM SUPER

NEVER IN A SLUMBER, NEVER IN A STUPOR

I AM A STRIVER, NOT AN IDLER

BEING AMBITIOUS IS MY DESIRE

I AM A WARRIOR

I DON'T LIKE NEGATIVE BARRIERS

I SHARE KNOWLEDGE, I AM A POSITIVE CARRIER

I AM A MOTHER, I EMPOWER

I BELIEVE IN GOD, I BELIEVE IN JEHOVAH

I BRING LOVE

PEACE AND UNITY

FOREVER

THE WILD CHILD

1977 THE DEATH BIKERS CAME, RIDING IN THE NIGHT

WITH KILLING ON THEIR MIND, THEY CHALLENGED A GUNFIGHT

THEY SHOOT UP THE AREA, THEY SHOT AT HER SON

THAT DREADFUL SATURDAY NIGHT IN CENTRAL KINGSTON

A BULLET PIERCE HIS FOREHEAD, AS HE TRIED TO HIDE

HE LATER DIED, IN THE GARRISON CALLED SOUTHSIDE

HIS MOTHER HEARD THE NEWS, AND SHE SIGHED NO, SHE DID NOT CRY

SHE WARNED HIM ABOUT THE MEAN STREETS

THE GUNS, AND CRIMES

SHE TOLD HIM, "DON'T GET INVOLVED WITH BADNESS, HAVE NO GANG TIES"

BUT HE DIDN'T LISTEN, AND NO HE DIDN'T

DO WHAT WAS RIGHT

TOO LATE, NOW THE YOUNG MAN HAS MET HIS DEMISE
HIS GIRLFRIEND WAS PREGNANT, SHE WAS WITH CHILD
SHE OFTEN WONDERED HOW SHE WOULD SURVIVE
AND TO THE UNBORN BABY, WHO WOULD PROVIDE?
MANY ASKED, HIS MOM WHY SHE DIDN'T SHOW SORROW WHEN HER SON DIED
SHE REPLIED, "MY DISTRESS IS NOT SHOWN ON THE OUTSIDE
BUT DEEP IN MY HEART, DEEP INSIDE
I LOVED HIM, HE WAS MY OFFSPRING, HE WAS MY CHILD
'I TRIED MY VERY BEST; I MADE MANY A SACRIFICE
AND I TRIED TO GIVE HIM A GOOD LIFE
THERE WAS NO FATHER FOR HIM TO IDOLIZE
SHE PRAYED, HIS UNBORN SON, HER GRANDCHILD
HE WOULDN'T DUPLICATE HIS FATHER'S LIFE
THAT'S THE SAD STORY OF MY BROTHER
HIS NAME WAS GUY

I AM PUZZLED

TERRIBLE ATROCITIES, HAPPENED TO YOU

IN WORLD WAR TWO

WHEN HITLER MURDERED

SIX MILLION OF YOU, SIX MILLION JEWS

THE NAZIS SEIZED YOUR HOMES

YOUR WEALTH AND YOUR LAND

I THOUGHT YOU WOULD BE MORE EMPATHETIC

TO OTHER POPULATION

I THOUGHT YOU WOULD UNDERSTAND THE PLIGHT

OF A DISENFRANCHISED NATION

WHAT HAPPENED TO YOU, THE JEW

SHOULD NEVER BE REPEATED ON ANY HUMAN

SO, WHY ARE YOU NOW COMMITTING SUCH ATROCITIES?

AGAINST THE PALESTINIAN

IN 1948 THE JEWISH PEOPLE

MOSTLY EUROPEANS

SETTLED IN THE MIDDLE EAST, NOW ISRAEL

IN WHAT THEY CALLED THE PROMISED LAND

WHICH WAS ALREADY OCCUPIED

BY THE ARABS-THE PALESTINIAN

THE LAND WAS VAST ENOUGH

FOR THE EXISTENCE OF THE TWO NATIONS

BUT ONE LEADER REJECTED, WHILE THE OTHER ACCEPTED

THE PARTITION PLAN

NOW THERE ARE BOMBINGS

THERE ARE KILLINGS AND RETALIATION

ONE COUNTRY IS STATELESS, ONE IS A STATE

ONE BELIEVES IN TORAH, THE OTHER

THE QURAN

WITH ALL THAT RELIGION, BETWEEN THE TWO CLANS

WHY CAN'T PEACE BE ACHIEVED IN THAT REGION?

Discrimination

SHE HAD THE RIGHT ATTITUDE

SHE WANTED TO EXCEL, AND BE

NOBODY'S FOOL

SO, SHE WENT BACK TO SCHOOL

TO GAIN ADVANCED SKILLS AND TOOLS

JOBS WERE ADVERTISED, ONLINE

SHE APPLIED

THEY SAY SHE WAS MORE THAN QUALIFIED

SHE WAS EXPERIENCED, SHE HAD THE CORRECT EDUCATION

SHE CAME WITH THE HIGHEST RECOMMENDATIONS

PREVIOUS EMPLOYERS GAVE FAVORABLE COMMENDATIONS

SHE PROJECTED SELF-CONFIDENCE, SHE HAD MOTIVATION

ON PAPER, SHE WAS THE RIGHT CANDIDATE FOR THE OCCUPATION

THEN THE MANAGERS MET HER IN PERSON THEY WERE CERTAIN

WITHOUT HESITATION, THEY MADE

A DETERMINATION

SHE WASN'T THE RIGHT FIT FOR THE CORPORATION

BECAUSE SHE HAD THE

WRONG PIGMENTATION

SHE WASN'T CAUCASIAN

"I Speak. You Read" available online at www.amazon.com.

About the Author

Charmaine Allwood-Hanson can be called a poet extraordinaire. She is a brilliant and talented poet, writing awe-inspiring, poignant, and relatable poems. Mrs. Allwood-Hanson, writes with passion and emotion, straight from the heart. Charmaine present to you in her new book titled "I Write, You Recite" poems which center around current events, topical issues, and life in general. The poems in "I Write, You Recite" are thought-provoking, inspiring, and witty. If you were amazed and enjoyed the lyrical contents, of her first book of poems, "I Speak, You Read" you will be equally gratified, reading, or reciting, "I Write, You Recite."

Charmaine Allwood Hanson was born in Kingston, Jamaica, and now resides in South Florida, with her husband Winston. She is also a mother of three, a grandmother, and a registered nurse by profession. She has been writing poems for eons, and is delighted to share her talent with the world, with her second book of poem aptly titled,

"I Write, You Recite."

Made in the USA
Middletown, DE
06 March 2023